★ ★ ★

UNSUNG HEROES

UNSUNG HEROES
Combat Nurses & Army Wives

By

LaVada "Rue"
Bishop Aquilina

TREGO-HILL
PUBLICATIONS

EL PASO • TEXAS

TREGO-HILL
PUBLICATIONS
—————
EL PASO • TEXAS

Contents

Map of the South Pacific
on page 34.

THIS BOOK IS DEDICATED TO
*my beloved husband Ray,
and to all my beautiful children
and grandchildren:
Rack, Dan, Debbie, Tim, Rusty,
"Lil" Danny, Kati, Susie,
Maddie, Bruce, and Rosie.*

*And to all whose lives
have so dearly touched mine—
without whom this story
would not have been possible.*

—Rue Aquilina

Preface

Heroes walk among us daily and usually go unsung. One such heroine was LaVada Bishop "Rue" Aquilina, "just a little ordinary girl from Arkansas." Her autobiography chronicles her life from early childhood during the Great Depression to her days as a young Army nurse in the Philippines during World War II. She describes her subsequent years as a civilian nurse and Army wife of career officer Ray Aquilina and as mother to their five children. Her fascinating life was "lived 'round the world" during one of the most interesting periods of history, the post World War II era. She weaves a colorful tapestry with her descriptions of their lives in such far off places as Japan and France. Their years in Athens, Greece, during the late 1960s under the reign of a brutal CIA-backed military dictatorship, saw danger and intrigue. The story is a good one, told from the perspective of a caring and compassionate woman. Rue Aquilina, devoted to her family and to all those whose lives so dearly touched hers, is truly an unsung hero.

She started the task of writing this book in the Spring of 1994. In June of 1995, however, she was diagnosed with pancreatic cancer. Knowing that she didn't have much time left, she set out to complete the remaining chapters. By August 1995, they were finished. Although she never saw the published book, one can take solace in the realization that this book represents her gift to everyone—her immortality.

Childhood Memories

THE DISTANCE from a farm in Prescott, Arkansas, to Papua, New Guinea, cannot be measured in miles. The only way I can calculate the true distance is to think in terms of light years. But, I made that journey more than fifty years ago when I served as an Army nurse in the South Pacific Theater of Operations.

I was born in Prescott, Arkansas. Although I came from what is known as a broken home, I do not think my family was any more unusual than other families. Broken homes abound in the United States. I was, perhaps, more fortunate than many children because I lived a great deal of time with my maternal grandparents. They showered me with love and affection and gave me the security I needed.

Nor was my childhood one of great deprivation and hardship. There was not a whole lot of money floating around, but neither was a wolf howling at the door. Perhaps I had holes in my stockings and my shoes were sometimes too small. I had shoes and I had stockings. Although my parents were divorced and my mother was more of an adolescent than a mother, I had my grandparents, Big Mama and Big Daddy, with whom

I lived, and had a family with whom I could visit and play and feel wanted.

For the time and place, my childhood was not extraordinary. A fine set of values were instilled in me throughout my childhood, and this was true despite the hardships inherent in growing up in rural Arkansas in the 1920s and 1930s.

My mother married when she was just sixteen, but I was not born until she was twenty. Five years later she divorced my father. She was a good-looking woman. She could play the piano and fiddle, she wore long skirts and lace-up boots and could dance the Charleston and the shimmy.

When I was in the fourth grade, we moved to the southern part of Arkansas. An oil boom was on and many people were moving south to get rich in the oil fields. My father's Aunt Ella and Uncle Jake Sallee owned a boarding house and my mother worked there. A lot of men worked in the oil fields and mother dated lots of them. She dated so much and often that a family conference was held regarding my little sister Betty Jo and me, and as a result, we were sent back to the farm to live with Big Mama and Big Daddy. I remember the farm. All kinds of vegetables, fruits and melons grew in the field below the big house on the hill. There was a large cotton field and black families lived there in small shacks, and they were the ones who planted and picked the cotton for Big Daddy. At night we smelled possums and sweet potatoes being cooked over open fires.

We had our happy times and our sorrows. When I was four years old, Big Mama's oldest daughter, Aunt Leola Mann, died in childbirth and left little twin boys. She also had three daughters, Sallie, Red, and Kitty Sue. They were too young to take on the responsibility of the twin babies so Big Mama and

Big Daddy took them home to care for them. I remember being in a large bedroom with a fire in the fireplace. Two cradles were in the middle of the room and the twins were in the cradles. I slept with Big Daddy and Betty Jo slept with Big Mama, and at night Big Daddy took care of Baby Lonnie and Big Mama took care of Baby Leo.

My memories are fragmented. I remember being in the front yard at the farm. I felt hot and cold; I was shaking. I had to find Big Mama! I got halfway up the steps and lost consciousness. I was found lying in the hot sun having seizures from high fever. Big Mama bathed me in cool water and gave me aspirin mashed up in water. I could hardly stand it!

Every morning at four o'clock Big Daddy got up and made a fire in the big wood stove in the kitchen. When the house was warm, he woke up Big Mama. I got up with her and sat behind the stove while she made soda biscuits, fried ham, sausage, potatoes, scrambled eggs and coffee. Big Daddy got up before daylight every morning because he liked to go down to the fields before it got too hot. Some of the black women came up to the big house every morning to clean and cook. At noon they would ring the bell that hung on a large oak tree out by the barn. The men working in the fields would come up and eat their lunch at long wooden tables in the back yard.

The next thing I remember was a small house in El Dorado, Arkansas. The house was on the railroad track and I learned how to spell Rock Island while watching the trains go by. My father worked for that railroad and was out of town a lot. Mother worked in a laundry and a young black girl named Nancy lived with us. She was not good to me. I would be in the front yard playing and she would come out and break a switch from a tree and switch my legs 'til I danced and cried.

I remember the sting and the hurt, and I wondered why she was hurting me.

I tried to go to school when I was five years old. I wanted to learn to read and write and knew I had to go to school to learn how to do that. I put on my best dress, socks and shoes. Then I took care to comb my straight, reddish blonde hair, but my bangs were too long; they got in my eyes. My freckles!! I hated them. When I got to school and went inside, I felt lost. I was alone and had no idea where to go. Two teachers noticed me wandering around and asked my name and how old I was. When I told them I was five, they were nice, but told me to go home and come back next year.

I remember the night Great Grandma Sara Jane Carruthers died. She was lying in a bed on a big feather mattress. Someone picked me up and held me over her so she could kiss me. She was my Indian grandmother. I can remember her rocking back and forth in a rocking chair and smoking her little corn cob pipe. She was always very quiet. My great grandfather Billy Carruthers was there with his shock of white hair, beautiful white teeth and long white beard.

The next memory is being back in the little house on the railroad track. Nancy, the black maid, was not there and I was glad. Most vividly, I recall being hungry and could not find anything to eat. I found a bag of flour and managed to light the gas oven. Then, I stood on a chair and mixed flour, water and salt and made little round biscuits. I baked them, but they were too hard to eat, so I doused them with vinegar which softened them, and Betty Jo and I ate them.

Life in El Dorado had its problems. My father did not pay the gas and light bills. Suddenly the gas and lights went off. When Mother got home, she hemmed my father in a kitchen corner and whipped him with a broom handle. He hollered, but she kept right on whipping him.

Not long after that, a model-T drove up and a big man got out, came into the yard and picked me up. It was Big Daddy, and I was so glad to see him. Mother packed two little tin suitcases and Big Daddy took Betty Jo and me back to the farm in Prescott. While I was at the farm, I learned my parents were being divorced.

And that was the year that I was five.

When I was six, I was old enough to go to school. Big Daddy took me to town in his buggy and bought me high top brown shoes and long stockings. With the neighborhood children, I walked one mile to the two-room schoolhouse in Thomasville. I loved my teacher, Miss Evelyn, and also loved learning to read. My bag lunches for school weren't very good. Big Mama didn't have much to fix for me—a couple of biscuits and some steak she had canned the year before, and there would usually be a baked sweet potato. Sometimes there would be an apple. It was a real treat when she made a fried fruit pie and put it in the bag.

I got into my share of mischief. Once I found Big Mama's Montgomery Ward catalog. I cut out a lot of paper dolls and played house. Later, I heard her looking for that catalog because she wanted to order something. Who cut up her catalog? It ended up in the outhouse.

Another time when I was bored, I decided to smoke some of Big Daddy's grapevine. With the grapevine and some of Big Mama's big kitchen matches stuffed into my overalls, I took off down through the pasture to the edge of the woods. I was not alone! Big Daddy's big black bull was nearby. When he began to snort and kick up his back hoofs, it was time to run.

I reached a tree and got up it fast. Since I couldn't go anywhere, I sat on a big limb and smoked the grapevine. The bull got tired and left, but I watched him carefully on the way home.

And then there were my crawdaddies. Some beautiful streams ran all the way through Big Daddy's pasture. I heard the water was good to drink, and I would get on my stomach and use my hands to scoop it up. It was cool and good and so clear you could see everything in it, especially some little things swimming and crawling around. My Uncle Fred Edwards told me they were crawdaddies and I could eat them, but they were strange looking things.

I decided to investigate. So, I got a cane fishing pole, fastened a safety pin on the line, put some of Big Mama's salt pork on it, and those crawdaddies actually nibbled the salt pork. I jerked the pole up quickly so they couldn't get off. Very carefully, I put them in my bucket of water. I let the big ones go—they were too big for me to handle. They had whiskers and big pinchers, and I didn't want anything to do with them, but took the smaller ones home and fried the tails in butter on Big Mama's wood stove. The white meat in the tails was tender and delicious, tasting like sweet lobster. No one else would eat them, but they didn't know what they were missing. It was my secret! They were mine alone!

In the summertime, we visited our Aunt Emma, Uncle Hugh, and our cousins, Mary Louise and Maud Elizabeth in Prescott. Aunt Emma worked in the Prescott Hardware Store, but during lunch-time she and Uncle Hugh taught us children how to play bridge. They also taught us manners—how to eat with our mouths closed and the correct way to use a knife and fork and also how to say grace.

On Saturdays, Big Daddy came in from the farm in his buggy, bringing all kinds of fresh vegetables, eggs, melons, fruit and milk from the farm. We were always glad to see him. We made tomato and mayo sandwiches from the wonderful tasting tomatoes.

Then, my mother married again. His name was Walter Urrey. He was a good-looking man and had a good job in the oil fields. When he was courting Mother, he was very good to Betty Jo and me, but later he changed. When they came to the farm to get us, my sister went to the storm cellar and locked herself in. She did not want to leave Big Mama and the farm. After much begging and pleading, she finally came out. At last, she agreed to go with us but hung onto Big Mama and cried and cried.

Our new house was in the oil field located in the woods at the very end of the road. It was small and Betty Jo and I slept on a mattress on the floor. It was very quiet except for the constant clacking of oil wells. A large torch burned day and night in the sandy front yard. We could leave our toys all over the place and were never bothered because no one ever came around. They always stayed right where we left them. The air was fragrant with the sweet smell of honeysuckle and dogwood blossoms. An oil pit was nearby, and I learned to swim in that pit.

School started and we walked about two miles through the woods and up the hill to catch the bus to school in Louann. After a few months, we moved to a larger house up the hill. There we had neighbors and children to play with. Betty Jo and I caught the "itchy" from those children, and I wanted to kill them. Big Mama and Big Daddy cured us when we went to the farm for the summer. Big Mama gave us sassafras tea baths and wrapped us up at night in molasses and sulfur. It felt dirty, but we were finally glad to be rid of the itch.

Later we moved from Louann to Smackover. There we had a bigger house and went to school in Smackover. My stepfather did not like us. We felt like we were in the way. He never hit us or abused us physically, but one way he showed his dislike was to refuse to allow us to eat at the table with him and Mother. My sister and I ate when he and Mother were through. Then we did the dishes and cleaned the kitchen.

On Saturdays, we liked to go to the Joy Theater to the movies. They had serials that were continued from one Saturday to the next. We did not have the money so I sold Mother's clothes hangers, but only got a penny for ten of them, and it was not enough. The nice man next door was an alcoholic, so I went through his garbage can and found empty liquor bottles. I took them to the Rickenbacker Hotel manager and he gave me ten cents for every bottle. We went to the picture show and stayed all day. There was a hot dog and hamburger stand next door to the Joy Theater, and I remember those wonderful aromas. We were hungry and our stomachs growled, but we didn't have the money to buy them.

My mother played the piano and arranged for me to take lessons, but because we didn't have a piano, I had to practice in the home of my teacher who lived next door. Sometimes it bothered everyone in the house when I went there to practice. The teacher liked me and gave me the lessons free and told everyone that I was her protégé. I don't know why because I never did become an accomplished pianist, even though I continued to study for years—even in high school for a credit.

This was the tenor of my life.

When school was out, Betty Jo and I went back to the farm in Prescott. Because my biological father was a railroad man, we automatically had free passes to ride the train. I packed our little tin suitcases, and we went back to Prescott. I decided we would stay there. In the fall, we went back to the little two-room schoolhouse. We had to walk the one mile in the rain, mud and the snow, but it didn't matter. I wanted to learn. I never stopped thinking about a better way of life, and with every inch of that one-mile walk to school, I knew that schooling would set me free.

When I finished the eighth grade, I had a problem. That was the last stop. There was no high school at Thomasville. Betty Jo was two years younger and had a place to go for two more years, but I did not.

Mother came to visit and said I might have to stay out of school for awhile. I was devastated! It seemed as if my life had ended before it had a chance to begin. All my dreams for the future were centered on doing something interesting with my life, and the opportunity would come only with education. I wanted out of the country, off the farm, and a better way of life.

The family talked it over and my mother said, "If you are really serious about an education, you will have to work for it." I was willing. She said I could move to Smackover and live with a family there. I was not yet twelve years old, but I would have to work for my keep and education. I took care of two little boys and did a certain amount of housework while I was going to school.

Every morning I dressed the older boy and held him by the hand as I walked him to school. When school was over, I rushed to his school and walked him home. Then I washed the day's dirty dishes and cleaned the bathroom. I also cleaned up on Saturday morning. The family had bridge parties every Friday night, and on Saturday morning there was a mess to clean up. This was the only way I could attend junior high school. I don't want to give the impression that these people were cruel or that I led a harsh life. Actually, these people were good to me and didn't expect me to do heavy chores. I was never expected to mop floors or do heavy work.

While I was living with this family, I began to menstruate. No one had ever told me anything about the reproductive processes, and I was convinced I had come down with a fatal and mysterious disease. A friend went with me to the bathroom at school and told me what was happening. She called my mother who brought me a sanitary belt and some Kotex.

In her book *From Nightingale to Eagle,* Major Edith A. Aynes comments at length on the lack of sex education given to young women. She states that when she was thirteen years old, she still did not know where babies came from or how they were made. Even young women who came from farms were ignorant of the most basic sex information. I guess I was one of those young women.

Major Aynes also said that before the changes brought about by World War II, nurses were "probably the most narrowly educated group of women with professional standing in the world." Throughout her book, she laments on the lack of education nurses received; she complained that most people thought of nurses as "trained" rather than "educated," and she attributed this to the fact that before 1940, many states did not require nurses to complete high school before entering nursing school.

Even before my teens, I knew that "education" was my way

out. True, we as a family were not starving and neither were we deprived, but we did live in a rural, somewhat backward area. All of us went to the movies, so therefore knew that life could be a lot more comfortable than the life we lived. I realized early that the only way I was ever going to get into the better and more comfortable life would be through school.

So I got my high school diploma.

But before that, other things happened in my life. Late one night, someone came knocking on the door. The lady of the house where I was living opened the door and was told that my stepfather, Walter Urrey, was dead. I was careful not to show my feelings, but how good that made me feel! I never did like him, and he was not nice to my sister and me. It seems he was riding in a car with another man and it went out of control and off a bridge at Smackover Creek. He was pinned in the front seat and drowned. The driver escaped with no apparent injuries.

But that was not the end of it. Six months later, whispers and rumors were going around about my mother, and were even printed in the newspapers. It was being said that Mother murdered my stepfather and his body was to be exhumed for examination. His brothers accused Mother of stabbing him and having his body dumped into the creek. But with the exhumation, there were no stab marks on his body. Then the brothers said Mother poisoned him. For financial reasons no analysis was made of the contents of his stomach, and Mother was absolved.

I was furious! I never saw my biological father and never saw much of my mother. She lived across town, and I knew where she lived. When needed, we could reach her. Even though we could not live with her, we knew she cared for us.

Besides, she had to work. Now she was working as a telephone operator at night.

Then we were living with her. She took a small two-room apartment, a duplex.

We still did not have a "normal" family life. My mother did not greet us when we came home from school, and we did not have lovingly prepared cooked meals. Instead, I learned how to open cans of pork and beans for me and my sister for supper. At eight o'clock at night, I would stand on a chair to reach the phone on the wall to call Mother at the telephone office to tell her we were going to bed. In the morning, I would get up and fix a breakfast of corn flakes for my sister and me, and we would go to school.

Being divorced and widowed did not stop Mother from dating. Now she was dating some man and wanted to marry him. I remember thinking, "Oh, my God! Not another stepfather!" But maybe this time it would be different. Maybe he would not be like the last one. He had been married, but his wife died, and he had an eight-year-old daughter. He had a big house out in the oil field, two cars and a big job. "Oh well," I thought. "She has had such a hard time. Maybe this one will work." Besides, if it didn't, we had an escape route. We could always go back to our grandparents.

Mother and her new husband went out West on their honeymoon. My sister and I were sent to stay with our father in El Dorado. By this time, he had a wife and three step-children. We did not know these people and therefore felt out of place—strange, unwanted, unknown. Not only that, the house was too small for so many people. It was dark and dreary, and I did not like it one bit. I could not understand why we had to stay there. It was not as though we were being given the "normal" family treatment. My father was always gone, working on the railroad, and his wife worked. We had no more supervision there than when we lived with Mother, who was working as a nighttime telephone operator.

It was a happy day when Mother and her new husband came to get us. We moved into the big house out in the oil field. It had a large torch in the front yard which burned day and night. It also had a gasoline pump out back so we never had to buy gasoline for the cars. I loved it. Our new step-father, whom we called Papa, was a kind man. He had a large goldfish pond made in the backyard and had his workers make a wonderful swimming pool on the property.

There was a problem. Mother didn't seem to care much for Papa's little girl. It was left to me to take care of her, do her bath, brush her teeth, brush her hair, get her ready for school, and hold her hand while we walked to the bus stop.

It was not really different from my life with the family in Smackover.

We needed clothes for school, but Mother didn't want to buy them for us. She got us only what she had to and took us to a second hand store and bought our shoes. It was hard for me to understand because now she had money to get us some nice things.

By this time I was in the tenth grade and studying commercial work: typing, shorthand and bookkeeping. I was very good and talented at this work, and it seemed to me a good office job would get me up in the world, and that is what I decided to do.

In my senior year, Mother had other plans for me. She decided I would be a nurse. I never liked chemistry and the sciences and was not good in those subjects. In fact, I hated them. We fussed, cursed and screamed! She won. I had no choice in the matter.

She had always wanted to be a nurse herself. Before she married her second husband, after she was divorced from my father, she had worked as a nurse's aide in Little Rock.

I was seventeen years old when I graduated high school. At that time, Mother placed me in the Warner Brown School of Nursing in El Dorado, Arkansas, which was run by the Catholic Sisters of Mercy.

Major Aynes described the nursing schools before World War II in her book. My experience bears out the truth of her remarks. Her concern was that nurses were being trained and not educated. I think this was true.

The nuns were nurses and they and the students ran the hospital like a convent or nunnery. At this particular time, most of the south was very anti-Catholic. Some of the local doctors violently objected to having a local hospital and nursing school run by the nuns, and some went as far as to threaten to burn it down.

As a first year student, I scrubbed bedpans, urinals, sterilized hospital rooms, learned how to make beds properly, bathe patients and change sheets while the patient was still in the bed. We worked from 7:00 A.M. to 7:00 P.M., with a break in the afternoons for classes. We learned bedside nursing with the patient as the focus of our attention.

We lived under strict and rigid rules. We were only allowed to go out on Saturdays and Sundays, but always had to be in by 9:30 at night. We didn't even have time to see a movie because we didn't get off duty until 7:00 P.M. One of the nuns always locked the front door precisely at 9:30 P.M., and if we were just coming in at that time, we would have to blow our breath at the nun so she could smell and detect the odors of alcohol or tobacco. One misstep and we were out!

All of the student nurses lived in the same house with the nuns. We also shared the bathrooms with them and came to know them quite well. I had heard they had shaven heads and was curious about that, but found out it was not true.

In our second year of training, we had to do twelve-hour night duty for thirty nights at a time. We had to get up at one o'clock in the afternoon for classes and that was hard. We were sleepy and tired most of that time.

It was 1939, and war was stirring in Europe. Hitler was overrunning some of the countries. The biggest shock for me was when I heard that Nazi troops had marched into France and taken control of Paris. The American Army started building up and some training was taking place in Arkansas. The nuns forbade the student nurses to have anything to do with the soldiers. They were sure we would be corrupted!

Finally, I graduated with ten classmates. In September 1941, we went to Little Rock and took the state board of nursing exams in the state capitol building. Just being in that building made me feel honored and important.

Now that I had passed my boards, I was qualified to practice as a registered nurse. Now what would I do? Jobs were not that plentiful, so I decided to do private duty. At that time, hospitals did not have intensive or coronary care units, and patients who were very sick or who had major surgery usually arranged to hire registered nurses to take care of them. The hours were from 7:00 A.M. until 7:00 P.M., or 7:00 P.M. until 7:00 A.M.—twelve hours a shift. For that we were paid $6.00. That was hardly enough to live on.

At that time, the Army was being brought up to strength.

The Japanese had attacked Pearl Harbor, and we were at war with both Germany and Japan. The services needed nurses. My best friend and I decided we would join the Army Nurse Corps. Mother objected violently. She was adamant. "No! You cannot join the Army."

I understand now. Major Aynes' book points out all too well the disrepute Army nurses were held in before World War II. Until Florence Nightingale went to the Crimea and opened a school for nurses, nurses were drawn from the lowest class of women. They were alcoholics, prostitutes, drug addicts. Uneducated women were nurses.

Fathers actually forbade their daughters to become nurses. My mother, obviously, did not feel degraded if her daughter was a nurse. However, an Army nurse was a different matter. A nurse in Arkansas would be under the supervision of family and friends. Who knew whom her innocent daughter would meet in the Army? Soldiers did not have the best reputations. When I was in nursing school, we were not allowed to associate with them. In many towns and cities near Army camps during World War II, young women of good families were not allowed to mingle with the armed forces.

My idea of the outside world was not Arkansas, not even Little Rock, the big city! I wanted out and into the big world and therefore decided to be an airline stewardess. At that time, stewardesses had to be registered nurses. They also had to be petite. I met both requirements and applied for and was accepted by TWA. I was going to Kansas City to be trained.

But then, it was December 1941, and because of the Japanese bombing of Pearl Harbor, war had been declared. My roommate and I decided to go ahead and join the Army.

Mother was emphatic. "No! You cannot join the Army!"

Nothing would change her mind. I'm not sure why she didn't object so vehemently to the idea of my being a stewardess. Perhaps it was because she never knew pilots. But she thought she knew all about soldiers and was determined that I did not join the Army.

Then she went to Hot Springs on vacation to take the mineral baths, and while she was there, I joined the Army.

That was the beginning of my tour in the Army Nurse Corps.

Chapter 2

Army Nurse Corps, World War II and Ray

W HEN I JOINED the Army Nurse Corps in June 1942, the United States was fighting a war on several fronts. In the European Theater of Operations, the allied forces were preparing for the invasion of the European Continent and Africa. The war in Africa was being fought, but it was far away, and the European invasion was still two years in the future. But the war in the South Pacific was real, and the conditions under which men were fighting were almost unreal. New Guinea was probably the most important battlefield in the South Pacific. The Japanese had taken it in 1942, intending to use it as a springboard for the invasion of Australia. Also, the Allies needed to recapture the island so that it not only would block the Japanese from Australia, but it also would serve as the Allies' springboard to retake the Philippines and for the invasion of Japan. MacArthur's strategy was not to take each island held by the Japanese, but to capture strategic islands and isolate the others by bypassing them. This strategy proved successful, but it took almost four years of desperate fighting to win back the South Pacific.

Every history of the war in the Pacific notes that the Japanese were not the most difficult enemy to face. New Guinea is the second largest island in the world, and it is divided by the Owen Stanley Mountain Range. The thick jungle vegetation and steep gorges of the mountains made transportation and fighting difficult and sometimes almost impossible. To add to the difficulty, the rainfall in the area sometimes reached three hundred inches per year, and was never less than one hundred fifty inches per year.

The climate and geography of New Guinea accounted for as many, if not more, casualties than the Japanese guns. Historians agree that the allied armies were ravaged by disease. Soldiers collapsed from the "debilitating" tropical heat and humidity; they shook violently from malarial chills or from being drenched in tropical downpours. Others simply went mad. As a matter of record, the neuropsychiatric rate for American soldiers was the highest in the Southwest Pacific Theater—almost forty-five per one thousand men.

The climate encouraged malaria, scrub typhus, dengue fever and tropical dysentery. These four illnesses alone caused four times as many casualties as did battle wounds. In addition, the nurses found the men suffering from illnesses that were new to them. Yaws, leprosy, bubonic plague, and cutaneous diphtheria were diseases with which they had little experience in their training and work in the United States. An Australian soldier summed up the situation when he was asked about conditions at Milne Bay. He answered, "Mosquitos, death adders, and crocodiles, blackwater fever. But don't worry mate. You'll be too busy ducking the bloody bombs to care much about the rest."

When I think back about all the death, diseases and all

the destruction that were present in the South Pacific during World War II, I find it striking that doctors, nurses and hospitals got short shrift in the histories of the War in the Pacific. Two or three brief mentions of the "medics" are about all. *The Army Nurse Corps: A Commemoration of World War II Service* is a small pamphlet put out by an unnamed publisher or government agency. This small pamphlet notes that "there is no single comprehensive history of the U.S. Army Nurse Corps, nor is there a volume in the Official United States Army in World War II series that deals with the corps." The compilers of the pamphlet say that the best way to get information about the Army nurses during World War II is to read the relatively few individual memoirs which have been published.

More than fifty thousand nurses served in the Army Nurse Corps during World War II. These nurses worked closer to the front lines than ever before. In the European and African Theaters, they were well within the lines of the "chain of evacuation" established by the Army Medical Department during the war. The nurses served under fire, in field hospitals, evacuation hospitals, on hospital trains, hospital ships, and as flight nurses on medical transports. The skill and dedication of these nurses contributed to the extremely low post-injury mortality rate among American military forces in every theater of war. So much so that overall, less than four percent of the American soldiers who received medical care in the field or underwent evacuation died from wounds or disease.

When I entered the Army Nurse Corps in June 1942, nurses were not really members of the Army. I was told that mine was a "relevant commission." I took this to mean that I had an "honorary" commission. What it really meant was that I did not get the same pay and allowances as the men who had

commissions that were not "relevant." We received one-half
the pay of a male second lieutenant. It was not until June
1944 that nurses were granted officers' commission with full
privileges, dependant allowances and equal pay.

That was the future. The immediate present, to me, was
June 1942. My friend, Margie Boyette, and I rode a bus
to Leesville, Louisiana, and reported to Camp Polk to be
inducted. We were given no orientation to Army life and
customs. It was not until July 1943, after I had been working
for a whole year, that a formal four-week training course for
all newly commissioned Army nurses was authorized. It
stressed Army organization, military customs and courtesies,
field sanitation, defense against air, chemical and mechanized
attack, personnel administration, military requisitions, corre-
spondence and property responsibility. More than twenty-
seven thousand newly inducted nurses went through this
training between July 1943 and September 1945 and were
graduated from fifteen training centers offering this orientation. But that was not how it was in June 1942. When I
arrived at Camp Polk, Louisiana, I was put to work
immediately.

I walked into an outbreak of hepatitis that was decimating
the troops. It was like the plague which swept over 17th
Century England and Europe. Soldiers, officers and Army
nurses were dying. The Third Armored Division, which was
due to be deployed to North Africa for the invasion of
Germany, was ruined.

The powers that be in Washington, D.C., suspected there
had been some kind of sabotage at Camp Polk, and everyone
was being tested for something. I had to donate a urine
sample once a week. The FBI came in and placed agents

all over the hospital. They were looking and searching
for everything.

I was assigned to the ward with the sickest patients. Most
were dying, and my job was to keep a graphic chart on these
terminally ill patients. I was told that someone at Walter Reed
Army Medical Center in Washington, D.C., was using these
charts to help understand the nature and treatment of hepatitis. In 1942, no one knew how to treat this illness, and it was
often terminal. The charts I kept on these patients were several
feet in length, and when a patient died, the chart was rolled
up and sent to Walter Reed Hospital. I hope that my work did
something to help find a treatment for hepatitis.

As for the reason for the outbreak, it was discovered that all
the troops alerted to go to North Africa and Italy had received
contaminated shots for yellow fever, but to my knowledge, no
one ever knew what contaminated the serum.

At Camp Polk, I worked with nurses and doctors from all
over the United States. I came from a small town in Arkansas,
and most of the places these people came from were just
names to me—names in history and geography books and
names in newspapers and magazines. Now, I was meeting
people who actually lived in those places and began to learn
a lot that I never dreamed of in Arkansas.

Interesting as it was to meet people from all over the United
States, even more interesting was the work I was doing. Where
I came from, registered nurses were referred to as "trained
nurses." In her book *From Nightingale to Eagle*, Edith A.
Aynes makes a point of differentiating between the "trained"
nurse and the "educated" nurse. She was all for the "educated"
nurse, and my education began at Camp Polk. I think I was as
good a trained nurse as ever went into the Army Nurse Corps.

I knew how to take care of patients and how to follow instructions. But, I also found that I had the capacity to develop beyond the "training." I think the charts I kept for the hepatitis epidemic were among the first signs that I was growing beyond the "training."

Before World War II, nurses took care of the patients, and that was all. They were taught to respect doctors as if they were god-almighties themselves, and when they entered the nurses' station, the nurses had to get out of their chairs immediately, stand to attention, and let them have their chairs— no matter how busy they were working on the patients' charts.

During World War II, nurses continued to take care of patients but began to expand beyond the narrow limits of the accepted definition of "nurse." Procedures like drawing blood, setting up IVs and blood transfusions were new to nurses, but they quickly adapted to new requirements on the job. At Camp Polk, I worked on an officers' ward and had some young doctors for patients. Every morning I had to draw their blood and, in the beginning, I was not sure of myself. Some of the young doctors realized it, jumped out of their beds and showed me how to draw blood. I became quite expert.

At Camp Polk, I met situations that I knew about but had not actually experienced. There was a problem with venereal disease among the soldiers. We had a urologist who was determined to find the women in the area who were infecting and spreading these diseases to the young soldiers. Sometimes the soldiers refused to tell who had infected them, so the doctor played detective himself. He had the soldiers watched and sometimes caught them in the act, and had the women arrested. Then, they would be tested, and the doctor found out they were rampantly spreading gonorrhea and syphilis.

They would be isolated and treated, and that solved the problem for awhile.

At Camp Polk, my good friend, Emily Lewis, and I decided we would like to become flight nurses. We applied for flight training, and that meant we would have to go to Bowman Field, Louisville, Kentucky, for training. We had to do this secretly to get around our chief nurse, who didn't want to lose any of her nurses. So, we went behind her back and both of us were accepted. Then I came down with appendicitis and had to have my appendix removed and could not go with Emily for flight training. By the time I recovered, it was too late. She ended up a flight nurse in the European Theater of Operation and I went to New Guinea!

At Camp Polk, we lived in barracks. There were two bathrooms for twenty of us. We had to keep our rooms clean and neat. If we slept late and didn't have time to make the bed, and if one of the assistant chief nurses came around and discovered it, we were punished. We were not allowed to go off base, but if we did and got caught, we had extra duty or were called to the office of the chief nurse and were thoroughly reamed out. It was almost like being in nursing school. We considered ourselves professionals, but here we were still being treated like student nurses. We had to be careful and very respectful because now we had to think about our efficiency reports and possible future promotions.

At Camp Polk, we worked long hours. We were doing twelve-hour shifts. When we were on night duty, we worked thirty nights straight. We worked hard but sometimes did have time off. I remember when Bob Hope entertained us. He came with Frances Langford and a comic named Jerry Colona. Frances Langford sang some of our favorite songs, and I remember what a beautiful voice she had.

Then there were dates—lots of dates. I was fascinated by all the people from different parts of the country. Here I was a simple country girl from Arkansas going out with guys from New York, Virginia, Texas, California—the whole United States.

It was war time, and any young woman could have two or three dates a night if she wanted to. She could go out every night. Sometimes I would be tired and when I was asked, I would decline and say I had just washed my hair. Sometimes I would lie and say I had another date. Besides, I had to be careful. Some of the men were married! We could usually find out from the other young officers who worked with them.

One night in September 1943, I went to the Officers' Club on a blind date as a favor for a nurse friend of mine. As I was dancing with my date, someone tapped him on the shoulder and asked if he could cut in. At that time, there were many young officers and not very many women around. Therefore, cutting in on the dance floor was accepted. When he asked my name, he was surprised, and said he was supposed to have a date with me that night. It was the first time I knew about it. I never heard of First Lieutenant Ray Aquilina before— but thought he was pretty neat, and a real good dancer.

It was one of those things. He had a friend, Captain Wes Hoffman, an MSC Officer with our hospital. He was supposed to get Ray a blind date with a good dancer, and he told Ray he knew two girls—an Army nurse and a clerk typist in the hospital admitting office. Wes thought I was still on night duty so he arranged for Ray to have a date with the clerk typist. But she went horseback riding and fell and broke her leg. Ray went to the club alone and that is when we met on the dance floor. He persuaded me to slip off to the other Officers' Club. When he took me home to the nurses' quarters, he kissed me good night but did not ask to see me again.

The next night, he called and asked to see me. I told him I already had a date, and it was true. No woman I knew at Camp Polk had to stay home because she had not been asked out. He asked for Monday, Tuesday, Wednesday, and I finally gave in. I agreed to let him take me out to dinner and dancing in Leesville.

After that, I saw him every night for two weeks, and then he asked me to marry him. I thought this was pretty fast. I knew nothing about him except that he was Italian and was from Brooklyn, New York. I was so naive that I had to add the New York to Brooklyn. I was always curious about New York. Most people in small town America are curious because New York carries a glamour and cachet and promise of excitement.

I had to seriously think about the idea of marrying someone I had known for such a short time. Even the glamour of New York had to be weighed against the fact that I knew very little about Ray. But he seemed to be stable, polite and learned. I decided he would probably be a good husband and provider. Maybe he would give me the security I had never had. If it didn't work out, I could always get a divorce. My mother did. But there was a war, and he was due to deploy to Europe. I knew I would be shipped somewhere. On the other hand, I liked him better than anyone else and decided I didn't want to lose him, so I said, "Yes."

With such short notice, we had to be married by a justice of the peace in Leesville, Louisiana. Ray's colonel, Clement Parrish, had a car, so he and his girl friend drove us to Shreveport, Louisiana to the Washington Youree Hotel, where we spent a weekend honeymoon.

After the honeymoon, we stayed in the home of Ray's captain, Steve Weston, and his wife, Capitola. There was a housing shortage, so we considered ourselves lucky to be able to stay with them.

Three weeks later, Ray was on his way to the European Theater of Operations—the ETO.

He went to England to train for Operation Overlord, the invasion of Normandy. Actually, he went in on the first day with the second wave of men who stormed the Normandy Omaha Beach on June 6, 1944. His unit was the air defense support for the 29th Infantry Division, and they stayed with the 29th most of the time during the war. But it was still September, 1943, and no one was a hero yet. We were just expendable cogs in the machine of war.

After Ray left, I was lonely. Even though we only had been married for a few weeks and I had known him for such a short time, I missed him and thought I could not stand it. But then, suddenly, I received orders. I was to join a hospital unit at Fort Sill, Oklahoma, to stage for movement overseas. We were not told where we were going—just somewhere overseas.

Overseas to the Southwest Pacific

IN FEBRUARY 1944, I went to Fort Sill, Oklahoma. There I was assigned temporary duty at the Fort Sill Army Hospital. We were issued all kinds of combat equipment, including a gas mask. We trained on the gas mask by running through a large tent. We had to run into the tent, quickly put on the mask, and get out as quickly as possible. I was not sure I would make it, but I did.

Our unit was made up of doctors, administrative officers and nurses from all over the United States. It was called a Cosmopolitan Unit. We had one hundred nurses and about fifty doctors. Our unit may have been cosmopolitan and I may have been in the Army for almost a year, but in many ways I was still a naive young girl from Arkansas. I never could decide which shocked me more—the married men in our unit dating the nurses, or the nurses dating the men they knew were married. Most of the doctors had their wives and children with them until we left Fort Sill on a troop train headed west. After that, maybe one or two of the doctors remembered they were married.

They knew we were going west and, therefore, figured it would be somewhere in the Pacific where there would be no white, civilized women except nurses for the duration of the war. When I found out our troop train was heading west, I felt like dying! My husband was in England by now, and I was on my way in the opposite direction to the other side of the world. I didn't know if I would ever see him again.

After rolling and bumping along for several days on the troop train, we reached Camp Stoneman, California.

At Camp Stoneman, we were issued tropical uniforms, given the usual shots, and waited and waited.

One evening some of the doctors came to the nurses' quarters and told us we would be shipping out soon. They said, "We're probably going someplace where we won't be able to get any alcoholic drinks." MacArthur had declared the Pacific dry. They said they were going to make a run into San Francisco that night to purchase booze and asked each one of us to make a $30.00 contribution—even if we didn't drink. Naturally, we wondered how they were going to get it over the ocean, but they said not to worry—they had a way.

Sometimes, when I think about that purchase, I find myself wondering. We had one hundred nurses in our unit and if each one of us was willing to ante up $30.00, the doctors would have $3,000.00 to use for liquor. They had enough to last until V-J Day in August 1945.

The doctors got the liquor over, and they managed to hide it. They hid it well. No liquor was allowed in any Army unit—but considering the geography and the plight of the soldiers, MacArthur never did find a way to dry up the Pacific.

Our stay at Camp Stoneman was brief. Late in the afternoon of March 8, 1944, we marched from Camp Stoneman to the docks where we boarded our ship. It was the SS Monterey, a former luxury cruise ship. It carried two large hospital units and five thousand troops.

I had never been on a ship before, and had never seen the ocean before, so I had no idea what was in store for me. As a matter of security, we had not been told where we were going. We suspected it would be somewhere in the South Pacific but knew nothing more.

Not knowing where we were going, I did not know what to expect. I thought it best to be prepared for everything. When I boarded the ship, I had a bedding roll, valpack, and footlocker. The footlocker was filled with Kotex and the valpack had my dress uniforms, nylons and dress shoes to wear with the uniforms. I even had an evening gown! None of this got worn before V-J Day. Where I was billeted, I hung the valpack on a nail and it remained unopened for two years.

On the very practical side, I also put in freckle cream (I had lots of freckles), cleaning creams, shampoo, soaps, and toothpaste. Underwear and pajamas completed my practical packing. Our tropical uniforms were khaki pants, shirts, boots and leggings. The leggings were new to me, but I was told they were necessary for protection against mosquitoes and all sorts of crawling things. We had brown seersucker wrap-around dresses that were to be worn at work, but we were not allowed to wear them because we were not supposed to excite the soldiers. There were one hundred of us and hundreds of soldiers. Since we were the only civilized women, the Army felt we had to be protected. We never wore the brown-striped dresses outside the nurses compound, but did wear them in our tent area and when we went to the showers and toilets.

On board ship, we wore the khaki pants. For shoes, I wore

brown loafers—not standard uniform. The chief nurse never noticed. She was too busy looking at my hair. I had lots of long blonde hair and plenty of freckles. Hair was not supposed to touch the collar of my uniform, and I always had a problem with it. It was a constant source of conflict with my chief nurse. She was tall, skinny and had a mouth full of bucked teeth and was a lot older than the rest of us. I tried to keep away from her!

The first night on board ship, we were served a wonderful dinner. The SS Monterey still had peacetime waiters and peacetime menus. We all sat at little round tables with white tablecloths, real silver and crystal. I ordered strawberry shortcake for dessert. After this voyage, the luxury was gone and the Monterey was completely converted into an regular troop ship.

Even though the full ship conversion had not been made, the Monterey was transporting troops several times the number of people usually carried on board. In addition, instead of following a fixed route of so many days to reach a certain port, the ship had to zigzag to stay out of the way of Japanese submarines. We were not traveling in a convoy. We were alone at sea. One result was a definite allocation of water resources. Long hot or cold showers were to be in memory only.

We were living in a large cabin that had formerly been used as a hospital ward and there were eighteen of us altogether. There was one bathroom with a shower, tub, and toilet. We were told we would be allowed only one canteen cup of fresh water a day and all bathing would be in salt water. We all got together and had a pow wow. We decided to fill the bathtub with fresh water, and every morning, each one of us would take one canteen cup of water to wash our faces and brush our teeth.

We sailed during the night after we were all asleep. When we awoke the next morning and went to the bathroom to get our cup of fresh water, it was not there! Someone had gotten up early and used our tub of fresh water to take a bath. It was gone! Who did it?? No one admitted it, but we had our suspicions, and we wanted to murder her.

We soon learned that bathing in salt water was not pleasant. Soap does not lather in it, and, after a shower, we felt as dirty and sticky as before. But one of us made a discovery. Colgate shaving cream will lather in salt water, so we went to the ship's small PX and bought all of the Colgate shaving cream the PX had. We never did find out what the men did for shaving cream.

Most of us had never been on a ship before. We discovered *mal de mer*. In spite of the fantastic food available, we had no appetite. Many of us fell victim to nausea and vomiting. Some could get out of their bunks only to get to the bathroom.

The nurses were not the only seasick passengers. We had five thousand troops on board and many of them were also sick. The hospital was on C deck and the troops were brought up from below. As usual, the nurses were put to work at once. Since my name now began with an "A," I was first on the roster. By this time, I, myself, was really sick. I passed out seasick pills to all the soldiers, took one myself, and crawled into a bunk. I told the soldiers to call me if they needed anything. I was as sick as they were.

Just about the time we got used to the zigging and zagging, we reached the China Straits and ran directly into a typhoon. At the moment of impact, some of us were sitting on the floor playing cards, and we slid across the room. Walking was dangerous, and we had to strap ourselves in the bunks. The ship groaned and pitched and tossed about, and we were sure we would capsize. Finally, the storm subsided and we could go back out on deck for fresh air. Someone sighted a foreign object in the ocean. "Oh, my God! It's a Japanese submarine! We're all dead!" But then we discovered it was just a school of flying fish.

After three weeks on the Monterey, we landed at Milne Bay, New Guinea.

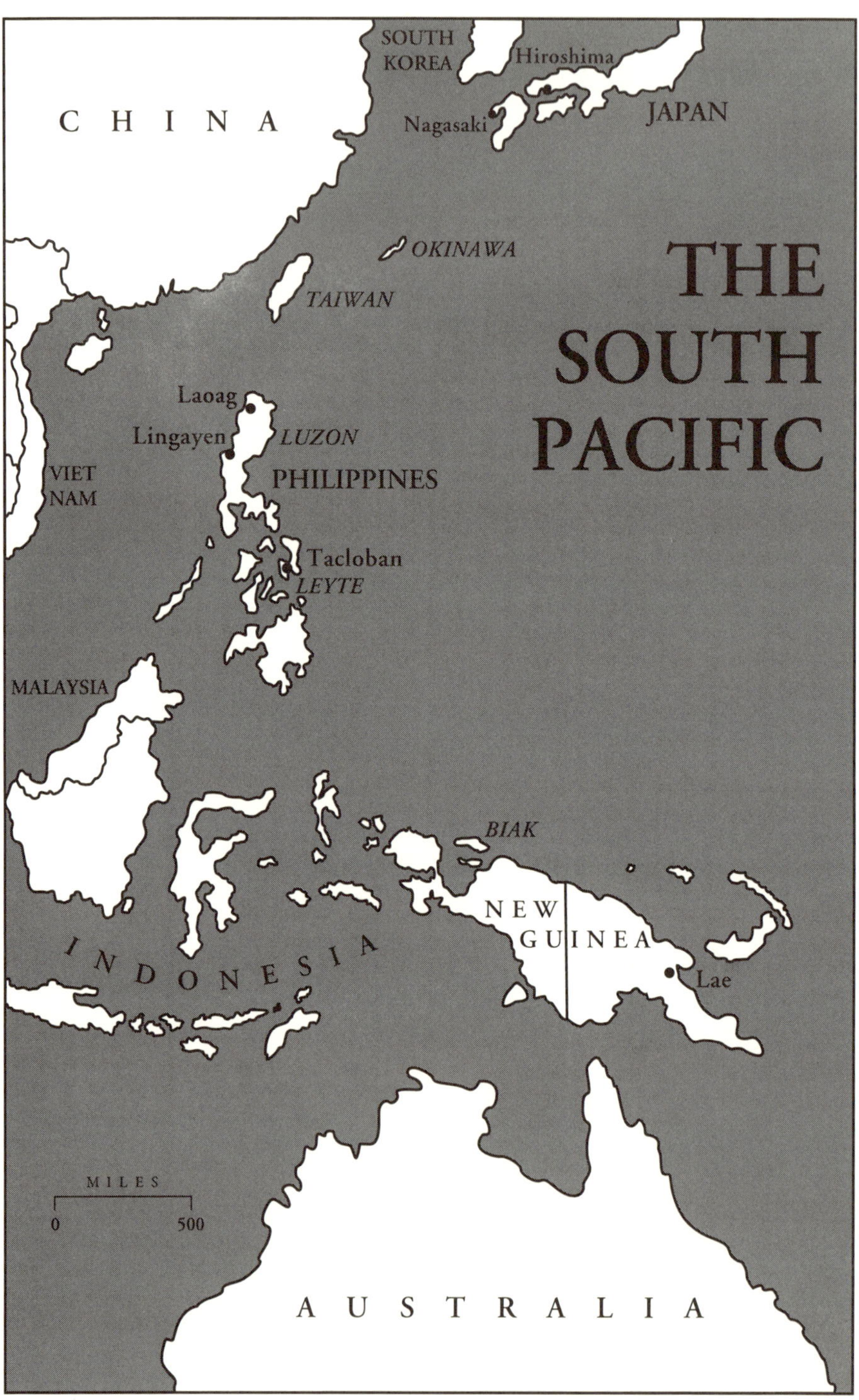

SOUTH KOREA
Hiroshima
CHINA
Nagasaki
JAPAN
OKINAWA
TAIWAN
THE SOUTH PACIFIC
Laoag
Lingayen
LUZON
PHILIPPINES
VIET NAM
Tacloban
LEYTE
MALAYSIA
BIAK
NEW GUINEA
INDONESIA
Lae
MILES
0
500
AUSTRALIA

New Guinea Jungles

WHEN WE LANDED at Milne Bay, New Guinea, we had no idea where we were. We could have been on the moon for all we knew.

The ship was so big, and since there were no marinas or docks, it had to anchor about two miles out at sea. We had to climb down rope ladders on the side of the ship and drop into LSTs (Landing Ship Tanks). We were dressed in fatigues with backpacks fastened on our backs with a pistol belt on which was fastened our mess kits and canteen cups. When I looked down at the ocean, I hesitated and thought, "What if I slip?" I was so loaded down, I was afraid I would sink to the bottom of the ocean and stay there.

When I had boarded the ship in San Francisco, I had a nice five by seven mirror in my backpack, but when I packed to debark, I couldn't fit the mirror into it, so a nice doctor offered to get it off for me. It was the last time I ever saw it. When I asked him for it after we landed, he said he lost it. I suspect that he wanted to keep it for himself. For the rest of my tour in the Pacific, I only had a small round shaving mirror that I could hook on a nail on a post in the tent.

After we dropped from the side of the ship into the LSTs, we were taken into the jungle to "tent city," which was set up in the middle of a coconut grove. In the center of the area was a lister bag with warm Halazone water, a community shower with buckets that had holes punched in them, and there was an 8-hole toilet inside a tent. There was no roof over the shower, so we frequently found soldiers looking down at us from the top of the mess hall. We raised hell! Our compound was surrounded by barbed wire, and guards with machine guns guarded us twenty-four hours a day. We were not allowed outside the compound without two or more armed guards.

Service in the South Pacific was not like service in the European Theater of Operations. Those who served in the ETO served in an area that had been settled for centuries— millennia. Perhaps Army life did not offer all the conveniences of home, but both men and women were in the ETO. The men were not starved for female companionship because they could mingle freely with the American women serving overseas (WAC, Red Cross, nurses) and the women of the allied nations.

The South Pacific was a different situation. In addition to the 100 nurses of the hospital unit, there were perhaps two or three Red Cross workers and that was it for companionship for the male troops. It was not possible for them to fraternize with the native women because there were none. Besides, New Guinea was not modernized. It was a stone age country and a land of head-hunters. Therefore, the Army felt it necessary to put the nurses in a guarded compound.

Sometimes we would hear blood-curdling screams. There would be a snake in one of the tents, and the guard would have to come in and shoot it. There were mosquitos and other insects which made it necessary and mandatory to wear leggings from five o'clock in the evening or be inside our cots with the mosquito netting tucked in well.

Our staff had moved ahead to Lae to set up our hospital. Since we were left behind until things were ready, we were loaned out to the other tent hospitals in the area.

MacArthur's plan for the South Pacific—to take strategic islands and starve out the rest—was beginning to work. Everyone has heard stories of Japanese who remained on these islands long after the war was over. But not all of them stayed on the islands. Some were captured and brought to our hospital area. We could tell how well MacArthur's policy was working by the condition of these Japanese prisoners. We were amazed by their emaciation and debilitation.

Our soldiers also suffered emaciation and tropical diseases as well as battle wounds. By the time I got there, New Guinea had been retaken by the allies, and our hospital was scheduled to be set up in Lae. However, as usual, we had to wait for orders, and while we waited, we worked.

We worked at the 18th Station Hospital, which was a tent hospital. I worked on a ward with patients who were eaten up with jungle rot. This was a skin rash that covered the whole body and oozed pus. No one knew what caused it, and no one knew how to treat it. The most we could do was to make the patient as comfortable as possible.

We made frames of wood and nailed rubber to them, making a bathtub. We filled the tub with water and soda bicarb every morning, then lifted the patients still wrapped in sheets and dunked them into this solution and let them soak until the sheets came loose. That was the only humane way we could change the sheets that had been frozen to their bodies with pus.

Most of our patients were in their early twenties; some in their late teens. Most people do not realize this war was fought and won by men who were mere teenage boys.

The soldiers who were wounded from invading the islands north of us were shipped back to Milne Bay. Besides being wounded, they came down with every known disease and several which were not then known.

Most of the jungle rot patients died right there in Milne Bay. When the fungus rot got into the bloodstreams, it killed them. Perhaps if we could have evacuated them to Guam or Hawaii, with a better climate, they could possibly have received more sophisticated treatment, and they could have been saved.

Then, there was the weather. It rained. It was a monsoon. It lasted for six weeks. It poured constantly—never a let-up. Our tents started to leak. We were sleeping on cots with no mattresses and no pillows. The cots were wet. I got out my bedding roll. I had a shower curtain in it and draped it over the frame of the cot that held a mosquito netting. That helped a little, but soon it, too, was full of holes from the downpour. My long blonde hair got wet. It wouldn't dry. It even mildewed. I had no choice. I had to cut it off really short.

The six weeks of constant downpour of rain ended with a hurricane. Tent poles swayed; coconuts flew through the air at the speed of 100 miles an hour. We had been warned not to stand under a coconut tree because if one fell and hit you on the head, your brains would get knocked out. I never thought of coconuts as a lethal weapon before, but I know about it now.

The hurricane tore up our shower and demolished our lister bag and toilet. Most of the tents were flattened, and, needless to say, no one got any sleep that night.

After the storm, the shower and toilet had to be rebuilt. While this was happening, we had to go to the jungle behind our area to bathe and wash our clothes in a stream. We took the clothes back to the tents and draped them over the ropes to dry. We had no irons, but that didn't matter. No one ironed clothes anyway. When we washed our hair and tried to bathe, we had to do so with our clothes on because New Guinea head-hunters were behind trees on one side of the stream and our guards were on the other side. Our guards had machine guns.

We were still in Milne Bay on June 6, 1944. The hospital area and nurses' compound were wired, and music played during the day. Sometimes the news was broadcast, and the invasion of Normandy was announced. I knew my husband was there, and now I had to wait for news. Mail came, but it was always several months old. It had to be sent from Europe, across the Atlantic Ocean to New York, across the United States, the Pacific Ocean to Australia, and from there to New Guinea. I never knew whether Ray was alive or dead. When I received a letter I would say, "Three months ago he was alive." I did not know until much later how actively Ray participated in the D-Day invasion. Finally, we received our orders to move. Our hospital in Lae was set up and ready for patients. As usual, because my name began with an "A," I was one of the first to go. At dawn we were loaded into trucks and taken to the airstrip. We were flown to Lae in C-47s piloted by Australians. They were good pilots, but too daring for me! They swopped down over the islands that were still held by the Japanese so that we could see them. It made me nervous, and I didn't care anything about seeing the Japanese. The plane had no seats—just a long bench running the length of the plane. Our bedding rolls and valpacks were all piled up in the middle of the floor, and we were lying around all of them. No one thought about seat belts then.

When we landed at the air strip in Lae, we were taken by Army trucks to our hospital area. It was a large hospital made of tin and screen wire. Our quarters were the same. Although we had showers and toilets, we did not have hot water, but the weather was so hot it didn't matter. Our tin and screen wire quarters were like ovens. I thought tents would have been better. We began working with casualties almost at once. The 100 nurses did everything. We bathed patients, fed them, brushed their teeth, changed bed linens and treated their wounds. We did all this without any of the technology that is available today. We used syringes to suck up solutions and irrigate open wounds, and gave them injections for pain and made them as comfortable as possible.

The wards were kept clean by corpsmen who helped feed the patients, did some of the heavy lifting and ran errands. Without the tender loving care, I am convinced many of our young patients would not have made it.

We worked twelve hour shifts with one day off a week. If we had heavy casualties, we worked until we were through. I never got a break. Sometimes I would think of Australia, and just long for two weeks leave where there were civilized people and I could eat a big steak, and drink a Coca-Cola with ice. But I never made it.

Working on the ward produced shocks I never dreamed of when I was going to nursing school. One night when I reported for duty, I was told a patient had died. I was told to tag his left ankle with his name and serial number. When I pulled back the sheet, I saw that he didn't have a left leg. When I got over my sorrow and shock, I tagged his right ankle.

Some patients were brought to us after being picked up in the jungles where they had been lying in the rain for several days. They usually had gangrenous wounds and they were also full of maggots. This was before the advent of antibiotics. Penicillin had just come on the scene, and there were sulfa drugs, but the broad spectrum antibiotics that we take for granted today simply did not exist. To make the soldiers more comfortable, we opened a can of ether and let it slowly drip on the maggots, putting them to sleep. That way the soldiers could get some rest, but when the maggots woke up, the pain began all over again. Maggots are actually supposed to help cleanse wounds, but the soldiers were driven crazy by them. Sometimes the patients were taken to surgery, and, under anesthesia, surgeons would scrape the wounds clean. Patients with gangrene had to have their limbs amputated. The penicillin we had was not long lasting, and it had to be mixed in a little bottle of sterile water. It only lasted for three hours, so we had to inject patients every three hours.

When stationed in the South Pacific, starting with Milne Bay, we found that our patients were debilitated as much from lack of proper food as from the conditions under which they lived, worked and fought. Not only did they have to endure the steaming humidity, the constant dampness, insects, snakes, the thick vegetation of the jungle, they also had to live on miserable rations. The food was terrible. We had K rations, C rations, and the rest was dehydrated. We would have considered Spam a luxury. For refreshment we had dehydrated lemonade. We called it battery acid and mixed it with water in a canteen cup, but we had no ice.

Australia was supposed to help feed us, but all we got from them was goat meat and silver beet tops. Hardly anyone could eat them. The hospital kitchen cooked for the patients and the staff, and everyone got the same food—goat meat, silver beet tops, and Vienna sausage. We had Vienna sausage for breakfast, barbecued Vienna sausage for lunch, and Vienna sausage hash for supper.

We did have some free time. We had no telephones or radios, and, of course, television was still in the future. We were lucky that our administration played nice music during the day on the public address system. Otherwise, there was not a whole lot we could do in our free time. But we did manage to enjoy various diversions.

We had an Officers' Club—in a tent of course. Wherever there were officers, you could be sure of an officer's club. Once a month there would be a dance. Some of our soldiers could play musical instruments, and they formed a dance band. It was good. The inspector general attended almost every dance, and his men were looking for alcohol. They would sit on the side and watch, and they could see the bottles the doctors brought out and knew it was there, but couldn't find it later when they came looking. Every Monday morning, they would appear on the scene and check our narcotics cabinets and measure every dram of grain alcohol. They never did find the cache of whiskey. Our doctors had it buried and no one knew where it was but them.

Once in a while, we would go to our outdoor movie, but it usually began to rain. We took ponchos and wrapped them around ourselves and just sat in the pouring rain and watched until the very end. Sometimes, USO entertainers came to Lae. I remember Jack Benny and his entourage. He had a little blond singer, Martha Tilton, who could belt out a song with the best of them. The beautiful actress Carol Landis came also. The performers roughed it in tents just the way we did. They usually left after two or three days and went on to their next performance. I remember feeling envious that they were free to go on their way, leaving us behind.

Everyone played cards. I learned to play bridge when I was a child and I continued to play. Sometimes the stress of our work crept into our leisure time. I remember one bridge game on a day when everyones' tempers were on edge. We usually had a table going most of the time. We were playing, as usual, when suddenly someone said, "I do wish you would cut the deck toward the dealer the way you're supposed to."

Shirley Berger answered, "There's no rule that says you should cut toward the dealer. It doesn't matter."

"Oh, yes, that's the rule," Dottie Creech chimed in.

"It is not," Shirley insisted. "There is no such rule. I'll prove it. I'll write to Mr. Charles Goren, who wrote the book on bridge, and ask him."

This was taking place in New Guinea at a time when a letter took at least six weeks to go in one direction! Nut Shirley wrote to Mr. Goren.

Three months later, she received a reply. Mr. Goren wrote, "Yes, that is the rule. You should cut toward the dealer so he knows how to pick up the deck." And he enclosed a bill for $10.00.

Shirley was furious! "Here I am, over here taking care of poor wounded soldiers, working nine to fourteen hours a day! He can't send me a bill. I won't pay him!" She said she would write to her cousin who was a lawyer in New York. He would know if she should pay Mr. Goren the $10.00.

Shirley wrote to her cousin. It took three months, but she finally got an answer. "Dear Shirley, Yes, Mr. Goren is a professional, and is entitled to charge whatever he wishes." And her cousin, the lawyer, had the audacity to enclose his bill to her for a $10.00 legal fee.

The only steady recreation we had was swimming. We were always near some kind of beach. In New Guinea, most of the beaches were of black sand because of the many volcanos. But even when we went to the beach to swim, we had to have armed escorts, so the chief nurse arranged for our guards with machine guns.

There were the to-be-expected romances and love affairs. In my small town country naiveté, I was shocked when the married doctors began pursuing the nurses. The romances and love affairs continued after we arrived at our destination and right on until the end of the war.

The Chief of Staff of surgery and the nurse in charge of the operating room had a hot affair that went on all during the war. Rumor had it, and we all believed it, that they were lucky because they had the keys to the operating room, and could use the operating table. I remember her well. She was certain he would leave and divorce his wife and marry her after the war, but it didn't happen. She was neither the first nor the last nurse to find herself on TDY with someone else's husband.

Not all of the nurses could take the wartime experiences. A few of them attempted suicide. One went berserk and cut her wrists. Another overdosed. The one who overdosed was a patient of mine. When she was being analyzed by the staff psychiatrist, he asked about her sex life. They all do that, don't they? She told him it was none of his business and hauled off and slapped his face.

We were at Lae about nine months. We stayed there longer than any place else because it was a convenient dropping off spot from other places.

Hattie Hays planted a watermelon seed behind our quarters. I have no idea where she got it. Someone probably sent it from the States. Anyway, it grew into a beautiful large watermelon, and when it was ripe, there was a watermelon bust. It was a real treat! The beautiful Mary Adams planted some sunflower seeds, and they grew all over the place. Zelda MacAlister had two pets. I don't know where they came from, but they were precious—a small dog and a kitty. She named them Josephine and Priscilla. When we left Lae, I don't remember what she did with them. Maybe some kind Australians in the area looked after them.

From time to time, we would have to get up before the sun, get our things ready, be loaded onto an Army truck and driven to the airstrip to be flown to another destination to be "loaned out."

In January 1945, we flew from Lae, New Guinea, to the island of Biak, the Dutch East Indies.

CHAPTER 5

105th General Hospital on Biak

W E BEGAN the new year of 1945 by packing up and moving. More and more of our troops were taking back the islands held by the Japanese to the north of New Guinea, and it was time for the medical personnel to move on to take care of the wounded.

We flew to the island of Biak. When we got there, we were assigned to various hospitals until our own hospital was ready.

Biak was a small coral island and quite different from what we had known in Lae. Coral is not easy to live on. Not much vegetation was in evidence, but otherwise the island was as hot and steamy as any other island in the South Pacific. Sometimes it would be 140 degrees in the shade inside our tents.

We could not get a drink from the lister bag at high noon because the water was hot enough to make tea or coffee—and we could not bathe until after the sun went down because the water was too hot.

Although we were on a coral island, there was dense jungle and snakes abounded. They were poisonous coral snakes. Sometimes when we woke in the morning, we found large snakes wrapped around our tent poles. The tents were built on stilts because of snakes crawling around on the ground.

When we left Lae for Biak, we knew we were not joining our hospital unit. Our unit was as far north in the Philippines as was feasible and was not yet ready for us. It was preparing for the big invasion of Japan.

On Biak, I was assigned to the 105th General Hospital, the Harvard Unit. I did not like it. They didn't seem to have enough supplies for the patients, no sheets for the cots, and the patients had to eat out of their mess kits. I was glad I was only there until I could rejoin my own hospital unit.

Living conditions on Biak were pretty grim. I lived with three other nurses. We slept on cots with a mosquito netting frame designed to keep out mosquitos, snakes and rats. We also had to take atabrine tablets every morning at breakfast. It was an anti-malaria drug, and everyone turned a bright orange color. After the war, my tent mate, Maryon Peterson, came down with a full blown case of malaria and suffered seizures for a long time.

In addition to everything else, while we were on Biak, we were bombed by the Japanese. They bombed the airstrip which was located within a mile of the hospital. Some of our soldiers were killed, and we received a lot of casualties from that bombing. I heard a couple of the air force nurses were killed also.

Through it all, we worked long shifts with very little time off. The islands up north of Biak were being retaken and we got the casualties. General MacArthur's troops were invading Leyte in the Philippines and we were receiving the casualties. In addition, we were beginning to receive some of our recovered prisoners of war. What a sad condition they were in.

I never saw anything like it. Emaciated and cadaverous, they had been abused and starved by the Japanese. We also received the American nurses who were prisoners. They were quiet and strange. We had a party for them in our recreation tent, but they were anti-social. They were shipped back to the States as soon as possible. I used to wonder why General MacArthur and his entourage escaped from Manila to Australia and left some of the nurses behind. I found out many years later from a Philippino guerrilla that some nurses left with MacArthur, and the ones left behind simply volunteered to stay.

In addition to the major inconveniences of life on a coral island, we had the minor problems history books often ignore. One evening, as the sun was going down, I went down the hill to the latrine. As I finished, a coral snake appeared in the doorway. I didn't know what to do, so I stood up on the wooden toilet and screamed for help. A nurse heard me and ran for our guard. He came and shot the snake. From then on, I used my helmet at night when I needed to go to the toilet.

Grim as life was, there was a lighter side—not often, but enough so that life was bearable. For one thing, we went swimming. In order to get to the sea, we had to swing like monkeys down a large vine. To get back up, we had to climb and that was a big job, but it was worth it because swimming was refreshing and relaxing.

One of our nurses, Dottie Creech, later wrote a letter reminding me of the time her bathing suit wore out. She had a red two-piece and a hole had worn through the seat. She wrote to her mother to send her a new suit as soon as possible. Not only was the mail three months in travel, but also when the letter got to the United States, it was dead of winter and her mother could not find a bathing suit anywhere. This was before department stores started to show beach wear in the winter. Dottie was not about to miss her swimming. She cut out a bathing suit from hospital sheets, using the material in double thickness, and made herself a bathing suit. We had a sewing machine in the operating room for making wrappers, and she used the machine. The suit was a little heavy in the water, but it worked.

Another good thing happened on the island of Biak. We got promoted. I joined the Army with "relevant" rank. That meant I got less money than officers of the same rank and no benefits such as pensions and dependant allowances. The nurses all received a blanket promotion at the same time. We became a part of the Army Table of Organization. Instead of having relevant rank, we had rank. I do not know the situation of other units, but I know that in my unit, no nurse was promoted. One day, a general visited the hospital unit and asked if nurses ever got promoted. Since promotions were possible, he wanted to know why we were all second lieutenants after more than a year on the job. The war was almost over when we finally got promoted.

Then the news came. Leyte had been recaptured by our military, and we were going to move there.

CHAPTER 6

Leyte, Luzon and the A Bomb

I N MAY 1945, we went to Leyte, and it was just like landing in heaven. There was beautiful green vegetation. Tall trees and lots of green grass were everywhere, and we could get tree-ripened bananas and pineapples. We were still living in tents. Sometimes we would have storms, and lightning would dance right through the middle of the tents. Sometimes the earth would shake, but we were much more comfortable here than we had been on any of the other islands. This was civilization. We were glad to be off the Stone-Age island of New Guinea. We were even able to hire Philippino girls to clean our tents, make up our cots, do our laundry, polish our shoes and find fresh fruit for us. Even more miraculous, in the small city of Tacloban, we could go to a beauty parlor. We found a photo studio and had our pictures taken. Looking at the pictures, we discovered what a mess we had become.

We had been flown to Leyte in C-47s. When we got there, I was assigned to the 118th General Hospital, the Johns Hopkins Unit. I worked in orthopedics. The orthopedic ward consisted of two connecting tents. Each tent held between twenty and forty patients. Not one of them could do a thing for themselves. Some had two legs in casts; some were amputees; others had one arm in a cast and the other in traction. Some were basket cases—they had no arms and no legs and they were rolled up into a fetal position and cried like little babies for their mothers. I remember one patient in a body cast. I could never understand why he kept rolling off his cot onto the ground. I finally got exasperated. We had to get two ward boys to pick him up and get him back on the cot. Things were particularly bad at night. Sometimes I would hear blood-curdling screams from one of the wards, and I could actually feel my hair crawl.

We were so busy we had no time to keep charts and records on the patients. We just had their names and serial numbers on one sheet of paper. We kept a narcotic book, and if we wanted to know when a patient received a shot, we just checked that book.

Another time I worked in a psychiatric hospital. Mine was an open ward—no one was violent. But some of the men suffered from nightmares—battle shock. Some had flashbacks that would trigger violence, and they would have to be moved to a closed, more secure ward.

The Army had a practical but at times cruel policy. The men were brought out of the jungle on stretchers. Because then we did not have helicopters, they were brought to us in ambulances. When they were well enough, they would air-evac back to the States. But air-evac would not take them if they had a temperature of 101 degrees, and one of our jobs was to get them into good enough shape to travel. Each patient boarding an air-evac plane had his temperature taken by a nurse before he was boarded, and if he had a fever, he was turned back. Our hearts went out to these young soldiers, because we knew it was tantamount to a death sentence. We always thought that by getting them out and to a better climate they might stand a chance.

We were finally ordered to proceed to our original hospital, the 35th General Hospital, which had been set up at San Fernando, La Union, Luzon, for the great invasion of Japan. It had three thousand beds, but not in tents this time. It was tin and screen wire.

We went north on the hospital ship Hope. On board we had a chance to rest and relax. We sat on the floor of the deck and played bridge or just rested and laid around. We knew the war was winding down because the ship sailed with all the lights on. At night, the beautiful white hospital ship looked like a Christmas tree. We loved it.

The war in Europe ended on May 7, 1945. I was on Leyte that day, but we had no big celebration. For us, the war was continuing. We were still fighting and the most vicious fighting in the world was in the Pacific.

We heard that some troops were going to be redeployed from Europe to the Pacific in the hopes of ending the war sooner. All our troops were to be thrown against the Japanese. My husband was in Paris and expected to be deployed to the Pacific. While he was waiting, he studied French language and civilization at the Sorbonne.

We could feel the war near its end. Our troops had all but wiped out the Japanese on the islands, and we were preparing for the invasion of Japan. It never happened. While we were being transported to northern Luzon, an announcement came over the public address system that some kind of powerful secret weapon had been dropped on Hiroshima in Japan. We had no idea what had happened, but were hoping for a quick surrender. Japan did not surrender, and we heard another bomb was dropped on Nagasaki. This time, we heard news of the surrender.

We were in San Fernando, La Union, Luzon, on V-J Day. My tent mate, Maryon Peterson, had a bottle of bourbon concealed in her valpack. She must have been carrying it with her during the whole war. When she heard the news, she opened the bottle, drank, and shared it with Donna Flahrety, Donna Blomquist, Ellen Berg, Peggy Harmon, and me. We all celebrated, but Peterson got so drunk she had to try to sober up sitting on the shower floor with water pouring over her, clothes and all. It would have been better if we had had some grapefruit juice and ice to go along with the bourbon.

We landed at Lingayan Gulf in the northern Philippines in August 1945. I had been in the South Pacific since March, 1944. The war was over, but our work was not. From the hospital ship Hope, we were loaded onto military trucks and driven miles north to our hospital unit. A dance was given in the mess hall to celebrate the reunion with our doctors and administrative officers. After all this time, there was a family-like bonding with everyone in our medical unit.

We were put to work as soon as we arrived. This time, we were nursing Philippino guerrillas. They had been jungle fighters, committing espionage, etc., against the Japanese troops. They were very sick—suffering from malnutrition, dysentery, and their wounds were not only gangrenous, but also full of maggots.

We had more leisure time here than at any time during the war. We heard of a beautiful and cool resort somewhere up in the mountains not far from us, so we decided to take a trip there. We heard that high-ranking Japanese officers went there to enjoy rest and recreation after they overran the Philippines. Our chief nurse arranged for transportation with armed guards. We were still kept under armed guard, even though the war was over. High up in the mountains, we reached a beautiful village called Bagio. We went sightseeing, ate lunch at a nice hotel, and shopped for Philippino silver filigree jewelry, place mats, etc. The visit had a dark side. We had been warned of the Huks. They traveled in gangs and were considered dangerous. We heard they were not very civilized and that they ate dogs.

In October 1945, rumors were flying about that we would be leaving and going home soon. A new group of nurses arrived from the States, and oh, how fresh and wholesome and generally terrific they looked! They were there to replace us. They stared at us. I knew what they were seeing. Skinny women, yellow from atabrine, women who had lived under primitive conditions for a year and a half, women who had almost forgotten what a pretty dress, a good hairdo and make-up could do for them. I even forgot how to use lipstick. Our replacements probably never gave this a thought, and we thought how lucky they were. They were coming into a stabilized area and would have the niceties we thought we would never see again.

Chapter 7

Going Home

WE WERE really going home. The Army transported us to Manila in Army trucks. I remember passing by Clark Air Force Base. In Manila, we were billeted in tents on a great sandy beach.

Manila had some beautiful homes and one was used as a club for us. I was amazed at the beautiful winding stairs and marble bathrooms. I had almost forgotten how the civilized world lived, and now here I was in luxury I had never known in my life! After two years in tents and jungles, I could hardly believe what I saw and touched.

We stayed in Manila while waiting for a ship to come in. After about three weeks, we boarded a very old hospital ship called the SS Emily Weder. I never did find out who Emily Weder was, but was overjoyed to be leaving. Some of the nurses were not so happy. Many of them could never get dates back home, and now they were leaving an area and atmosphere where they could pick almost any date they wanted. It was over, and they knew it.

We were instructed to get out our dress uniforms. We had not worn them in two years, but were told we would have to put them on when we debarked in California. They were wrinkled and smelled musty. I didn't want to wear mine. Since I had not worn anything but khaki pants and fatigues for so long, I didn't feel right in a skirt, nylons and Oxford shoes.

We left Manila in November 1945. The ship was much too slow for me. The food was mediocre and the weather bad. I did not have to work on this trip, but everyone was getting seasick. Several nurses caught colds and had trouble with their sinuses. We weren't used to cold weather. After a few days at sea, the ship broke down and we just floated around going nowhere. It was rumored that this was to be the last trip for the Emily Weder. I believed it. It was so cold out on deck, I could hardly stand it, but the old nurse in charge demanded that we stay outside most of the time. I don't know why. I enjoyed lying in my bunk and reading books from the ship's library and counting the days until I would get home and not have to deal with old cantankerous Army nurses any more.

After three weeks of misery at sea, we approached the California coast near Riverside. Blimps were floating around in the sky with "Welcome Home" messages and music. It was exciting.

We debarked and were put on buses for a short ride to Camp Anza near Riverside. We were met by Red Cross workers with cartons of milk and doughnuts. It was greatly appreciated, but what I really wanted was a Coca-Cola with ice.

After we arrived at the barracks and freshened up, we went to dinner. We were told we could have anything we wanted. We all ordered steaks and french fries, a head of lettuce, lots of cool sweet milk, and whatever else we could eat. I found

I could not eat as much as I used to because my stomach seemed to have shrunk. When I went to New Guinea I weighed one hundred and ten pounds. When I got back to California I weighed only eighty pounds. I never did get all the way back to one hundred and ten pounds, but enjoyed trying.

Ray had been back in the States one month and was waiting for my call at his home in Brooklyn. He was excited and wanted me to fly there immediately. He did not know there were no planes and did not realize that I first had to be separated from the service. I told him I had to go to San Antonio, Texas, to be separated, and then I wanted to visit my family in Smackover, Arkansas. He said he would take a train there to meet me and asked me to make reservations at the Gunther Hotel.

We rode a troop train from Riverside to Fort Sam Houston. We had to sit up for the entire trip and ate the same old C-rations on the train that we had eaten for two years in the Pacific. We were often sidetracked for fast passenger trains.

In San Antonio, we were billeted in barracks at Fort Sam Houston. We had private rooms and were treated wonderfully. We each had a staff car with a chauffeur at our disposal at all times. No one bothered us in any way, and we had complete freedom—except for the discharge processing paperwork.

I used my staff car and chauffeur to take me downtown to San Antonio to shop. I had plenty of money to spend on new clothes, and the first thing I bought was a beautiful pair of shoes. I loved shoes because when I was a kid, I was barefoot half the time. My new shoes had high heels. I tottered around, and my ankles turned and my knees knocked. I had to learn how to walk all over again.

The next thing I bought was a suit and some dresses, nice underwear, nylons, gloves, purses. I was starting from scratch—from inside out and from top to bottom. Then came pajamas, bathrobes, and make-up. I bought all the good make-up that I wanted, but I had to learn how to use lipstick all over again.

My discharge took about a week.

When I went to the Gunther Hotel to make reservations, I was told they were all filled up. I couldn't believe it! They had to have a room for me! This was where my husband could find me. The clerk was kind and understanding and called around and found a room at another hotel, and took a message to let Ray know where he could find me.

Ray was due to arrive at the train station at 8:00 o'clock that night, so I had my chauffeur drive me there. I asked him to wait for me. As I walked into the station, I heard the train pulling in and people started getting off. There were so many people, I started to get nervous. I didn't see Ray! What if I didn't recognize him!! It seemed that I hardly knew him. I might not even want him back. I panicked. I turned around and ran back outside, jumped into the car, and told the driver to take me back to the hotel. Ray would just have to find me.

At the hotel, I dismissed the driver and waited in my room for almost an hour. Then there was a knock at the door. I was so nervous, I almost didn't open it. But there was Ray standing there with a big smile on his face. I just stood there, looking at him with all his medals.

My first words were, "Your nose got bigger, and I have more bronze campaign stars than you." He quickly explained that five bronze campaign stars become one silver star, and he was wearing a silver star for all five campaigns in the ETO.

He hugged and kissed me and things were rather awkward. I was wondering what to do about this situation. I didn't feel the least bit attractive. I weighed eighty pounds and was yellow as an orange from two years of taking atabrine. My hair was short, and even though I was wearing a dress, stockings and high heels, I did not feel right. It had been two years since I had worn anything but khaki pants and high-top shoes. I was uncertain about the future—the immediate future, the near future, and the distant future—but mostly I was uncertain about the immediate moment. My husband seemed like a stranger! I thought about Tarzan and how he would react to civilization after life in the jungles, and almost wished I could go back and just wear fatigues and khaki pants, and swing on the jungle vines.

He sensed my nervousness and was very careful. He asked if I was hungry, and I said, "Yes." We had to walk down the street to find a restaurant, and I found walking difficult in the high heels. My ankles kept turning and I felt silly. Ray held on to me to keep me from falling.

I don't remember what I ate, but Ray ordered some wine, and after a couple of glasses, I relaxed a little.

Back at the hotel, I filled the tub with water, locked the door, and relaxed in a long, long bath. When I finished, I sat in a chair in the corner of the room and told him he could take his bath. He took a fast one, came out in his jockey shorts, and crawled into bed. He wanted to tell me about some of his experiences in the war, but I asked him not to bore me because I had more trouble fighting the mosquitos than he did against the Germans. He just smiled and kept his sense of humor.

Finally, I decided I was tired of sitting in the chair. I looked at him carefully, and he had rolled over and seemed to be sleeping. When I slipped into the other side of the bed, he was not asleep at all. He reached over and grabbed me. There was nothing I could do. I couldn't run down the hall crying, "Rape." After all, he was my husband.

The next morning we went out for breakfast. I was feeling a little more comfortable with him.

That night we boarded a train for Smackover, Arkansas, and a reunion with my family. The train was full of young soldiers, loud and rowdy, returning home. There was lots of singing, especially Texas songs. The trip lasted twenty-four hours. We sat up for the whole trip, and the only food we got was what we bought when the train stopped and we hopped into the station to buy a very fast sandwich.

We finally arrived in Smackover and were met at the station by Mother, Papa, my sister, Betty Jo, her husband Willie, and their three-year-old daughter, Betty Ann. They were all living together in the same house and were partners in business. They had pooled their monies and bought a supermarket.

Returning to the sleepy little Arkansas oil town and seeing my relatives again was great. One of the first things we did was to drive over to the farm at Prescott to see Big Mama and old maid Aunt Eva. Big Daddy had died in 1941. We did not know what Big Mama was going to think about my New York Yankee Italian husband, but she took a liking to him immediately. We also drove into town and visited with Aunt Emma, Uncle Hugh McDaniel, and my two favorite cousins, Mary Louise and Maud Elizabeth.

Time passed rapidly. Old friends came to see me and meet my good-looking Italian husband. We were there about two weeks before Ray had to report for duty at Fort Bliss, Texas.

I was to remain behind until he found a place to live, but Christmas 1945 was approaching, and I wanted to be with him for the holidays. We had been married more than two years, and had never spent a holiday together. Everyone was telling me what I should and should not do as if they knew a lot more than me. Mostly, they said, you must stay here until he finds a place for you to live. What will you do if you go there and get off the train and there is not a place for you to live? Stay here!

But I decided I was going to spend Christmas with my husband. I told him to find a place because I was coming. Once again, I had to ride the train for two days, but this time I had a sleeper and the train had a dining car. It was nice.

Even though Ray could not find an apartment, he made plans for me to come to El Paso. He made reservations at the Cortez Hotel. When he met me at the train station, we left my luggage at the hotel and went to the home of a family he had already met for a spaghetti dinner. He had established a good relationship with them and their two daughters who had been feeding him well before I got there.

Before I arrived in El Paso, Ray bought a used car. It was a Pontiac convertible. He had dipped into our savings, but we needed a car.

We lived in the hotel for about a week. Finally, we found a room in the home of a nice lady whose lawyer husband had recently died, and she did not want to live alone. The house was on Elm Street near Five Points, and we shared the bath and kitchen. The location turned out to be convenient. At that time, the Masonic Hospital was located about three blocks from Elm Street, and I went to work there on the day shift. I worked from 7:00 A.M. to 3:00 P.M., and most of the time I was exhausted. Every night, Ray wanted to go to Juarez to a supper club and dance until late. Staying out late became harder and harder, especially since I had to be up early for a strenuous day at the hospital. It was beginning to wear on me, and Ray told me to quit working.

Then one day, Ray bought some golf clubs. He was practicing his swing in the bedroom, hit the chandelier and smashed it. Our landlady was angry and said we had to move.

We found an apartment house on the corner of Nashville and Louisiana streets that rented only to officers. We got a small, two-room efficiency apartment, and everyone shared a shower and toilet down the hall. But there was a hitch. We had to live in a small cave-like place underneath the apartment house to wait for a vacancy upstairs. It was not quite as bad as it sounds. It looked good to us. The rent was only $8.50 a week. The management could be choosy—no pets, no children.

In the spring of 1946, Ray got sick. He went to the dispensary complaining of a sore throat. The doctors gave him sulfa pills and told him to drink plenty of fluids. He did, but since he was drilling troops in the hot sun, he perspired, thus losing the extra fluids he was drinking. The sulfa pills crystallized and cut his kidneys. Besides the damage to his kidneys, he suffered a strep throat. He stayed in bed over the weekend, and when he returned to work on Monday, he got worse. He was retaining fluids. By the next Saturday, he had gained more than thirty pounds! The next day was Easter Sunday, so I took him to William Beaumont Army Hospital. After getting the run-a-round, I put my foot down and demanded that he be admitted before he died! He was admitted to a ward with other officers, and the next day the doctors told me he was suffering from acute nephritis. He was put on complete bed rest and a salt-free diet. When I went in to see him the next day, I found him hooked up to an intravenous of saline and glucose solution. I was horrified! He was on a no-salt diet, and here he was receiving a quart of salt water in the vein! To me, this was quick murder. I disconnected it immediately and found the nurse. She admitted a mistake had been made.

The next day when I went to see Ray, he had been put into a private room and it was full of doctors. The chief came out and informed me that Ray had been placed on the critical list. A priest came and gave him the last rites. At this time, I discovered he had never changed the beneficiary on his GI insurance policy. His beloved mother was still the beneficiary. It got changed fast.

I visited him every day. When he got better and was bored, I taught him how to play bridge. Until that time, he thought cards were only for playing poker. He loved bridge from that moment on. Since I was alone and had nothing much to do with my time, I went to the PX for lunch. For dessert, I ate chocolate cake with ice cream. Still, I had trouble gaining weight. Every afternoon I went to the Officers' Club and spent the afternoon swimming and sunbathing. Ray was getting better, and I was having fun all by myself, doing anything I wanted to do. Shopping was on my agenda, too.

But then, Ray decided I should go back to work. He seemed to think I had too much leisure time. He wanted me to be busy. We really could use the extra money, so I went back to work. I didn't have much leisure time anymore. I took a job in the newborn nursery at the Southwestern General Hospital and cannot say that I enjoyed the work. The healthy crying babies drove me nuts, but my heart was torn when I heard the weak cries of the tiny sick ones. I did not like the job, but stayed and gave it my best.

Ray was getting better every day. He was finally given bathroom privileges, and when I visited him, he began feeling amorous and sexy. One day, he took me to the bathroom with him, and all I can say is that was one hell of a way to have sex!

By November, he was given a thirty-day sick leave. We took a trip to Juarez and bought Mexican serapes, leather purses, and other souvenirs for our families and drove to Arkansas and then on to New York. I finally got to meet Ray's family.

I was excited when we arrived in New York City, but Ray kept driving right through to Brooklyn. His family lived in a large yellow house on Crescent Street. They lived upstairs and rented the downstairs to another Italian family. Their youngest son, Rudy, lived with them and paid rent. It was the first time I heard of parents making their children pay rent.

Ray's sister, Dorothy, was married to Frank Abbate, a beauty operator, who had been a sergeant in the Army. They had a six-month-old son and lived in Queens. While we were there, she spent most of her days at the parents' home keeping us company. I remember how bitter cold it was. I had never been any place that was so cold!

The visit had some surprises for me. My mother-in-law told me how happy they were that Raymond married me, because he always brought home very beautiful girls, and they were afraid he might marry one of them and be manipulated by their beauty. I got the idea they didn't think I was pretty and were relieved.

I wanted to be friends with my in-laws, but had a hard time understanding them. They were from a completely different culture, and I had a hard time adjusting to their ideas. His mother frequently reminded him that she gave him life and he should not ever forget it.

While we were visiting in New York, we never went anywhere alone. One day Ray wanted to take me into the city to see the Rockettes at Radio City Music Hall. We left the car at the house and walked half a mile to the subway. We rode it into the city—a new experience for me. His mother came with us. We ate dinner in a Chinese restaurant because his mother loved Chinese food. When we went to the theater, I put on my glasses to see a little better. I was just a little nearsighted and didn't have to wear them all the time. This seemed to disturb Ray's mother. When we got back home from the theater, she announced to the whole family that I had to wear glasses. She made it seem that wearing glasses made me damaged goods. Then the whole family began to worry and fret about whether or not our children would have bad eyesight and have to wear glasses.

We stayed in Brooklyn for two weeks. During that time, I felt as though I was on constant display. All of the relatives and friends came to see Raymond's blond, freckled, southern wife.

In that two weeks, I wanted to shop. I had saved my money. I wanted to buy some nice things in New York City to take back to Fort Bliss with me. Ray's sister volunteered to leave her baby with her mother and take me shopping because she knew the good places to shop. I was told she was the smartest shopper in the world. She took me to every tacky, second-class store she could find. I couldn't find anything I liked. We would run around all day, and I would be completely exhausted at the end of the day and come back with nothing. After all, I knew quality when I saw it, and I knew what I liked and didn't like. At the end of our shopping spree, I still had my money.

I had a quiet and serious talk with Ray and told him I wanted him to go with me into the city to look for something, and he did. We went to Fifth Avenue—B. Altman and Co., Bergdorf Goodman, and Saks Fifth Avenue. That was where I found what I wanted to buy. I got some very nice suits—the sort of thing I needed as a young Army wife for teas and military social affairs. Ray's family was dying to see what I had bought. When they saw my purchases, they sniffed and said they would have taken me to Fifth Avenue if they had known that was what I wanted.

Those were the longest two weeks of my life!

When we got back to El Paso, Ray checked back into the hospital, and I went back to work in the newborn nursery to make up for the money we had spent in New York. Then Ray put our name on a list for a new Buick convertible. At that time you couldn't just walk into an automobile agency and buy a car off the floor. You had to wait. He sold the Pontiac and bought a 1937 Plymouth that looked like a model-T Ford. I admit I was embarrassed to be seen in it, but then, it was only temporary until we could get the new Buick convertible.

Ray had been on sick leave, and now he was discharged from the hospital and back to duty. One day in December 1946, he came home and said, "Our unit is being moved to Fort Ord, California." We were still waiting for the new Buick, and he decided to stay on the list. But we had to drive to California with everything we owned packed in a foot-locker and stowed in the Plymouth.

At Fort Ord, housing was hard to find. Nothing was

available for lieutenants on post. We found a very rustic cabin in Carmel owned by a Catholic priest. The only drawback was that it had no stove in the kitchen, and, according to the rules, we could not have a hot plate, so I could not cook. But I did have an electric broiler combination that I plugged in to make toast.

One morning, Ray had to be at the train station at four o'clock to meet his troops coming in from Fort Bliss. I slept unusually late that morning, and when I went to the kitchen to make some toast, I felt sick and nauseated. I was dizzy but managed to get back to bed before I fainted. When Ray came home from work, I was still in bed and had not done any unpacking. When he saw I was still in bed, he got angry! He said, "What in the hell are you doing still in bed?" I said, "I don't know what's the matter, but I can't stand up." He said, "You haven't had anything to eat all day. Get dressed. I'll take you downtown, and we'll get something into your stomach."

I managed to get dressed. He took me to a restaurant, and we ate. Then he said I needed some fresh air and should walk for awhile. He dragged me up and down the streets of Carmel in the cold air. I could hardly stand on my feet I was so weak and still dizzy.

The next morning was Sunday and I was feeling better. We went out to eat and suddenly I noticed a large swelling inside my left wrist. The lump was the size of a large marble. I realized that something poisonous must have bitten me in my sleep.

We decided to move and found a nice motel in Monterey at the David Avenue Motor Courts where several other officers and their families lived. It was the nicest place we had ever lived in since we were married. It had a small living room with fireplace, small kitchen, bedroom and bathroom. The rent was $20.00 a week.

I decided to go back to work. I found a job in a nice little hospital in Monterey, and everyone was very pleasant to work with. I drove the old Plymouth and Ray rode to work with another officer at Fort Ord. One day on my way to work, a wheel came off the car. Because I had to be at work at 7:00 A.M., it was very early in the morning, and I walked up and down the street ringing doorbells to call a wrecker. At that hour in the morning, it was hard to get someone to answer the door, but finally a nice man opened his door and let me use his phone. I believe he let me in his house because I was wearing a white nurse's uniform.

Shortly after that, I found out I was pregnant. It was February 1947. I suffered from morning sickness every day and had no appetite. Ray was so excited and happy that I was pregnant. He didn't want anything to happen to me, so he told me to quit work immediately. I didn't feel like cooking or keeping house and certainly didn't feel like socializing, so I asked Ray if I could go home to Arkansas to wait and have the baby. He agreed. I flew to Little Rock, and Mother and Papa picked me up at the airport and drove me back home to Smackover.

At Smackover, I made an appointment with our family doctor. He would deliver my baby. I had known him all my life and trusted him entirely. He did not think pregnant women should lie around and do nothing so insisted I go to work for him. He had an office with a small clinic in the back where he did minor surgeries. My job was to assist him with his surgeries. He had another nurse who ran the office.

When I began feeling better, I started wishing I had stayed

in California with Ray. I missed him and things were kind of messy here in Arkansas. I went two weeks overdue. I didn't think I would ever have this baby. I was impatient. Finally, the baby boy was born November 3, 1947.

While I was in Arkansas, Ray had been transferred back to Fort Bliss, Texas. When the baby was six weeks old, Ray drove to Arkansas in the new black Buick convertible to get us. At the same time, his mother and father rode a train from New York to Smackover. They visited for two weeks and liked Arkansas. One of the first things they said to me was, "Please forgive us. When we heard Raymond was marrying a girl from Arkansas, the first thing we thought of was Tobacco Road."

His folks got along very well with my folks, and the visit was very pleasant for everyone. They seemed to be quite fond of their new grandson, but were amused because when the baby cried, I picked him up.

Finally, we drove back to El Paso in the black Buick convertible. While we were in El Paso, Ray got orders for Japan!

WALKING DOWN that gangplank marked the end of what I like to think of as the second phase of my life. My childhood, girlhood and education had taken place in a small town in Arkansas. I was trained to be a nurse in the old fashioned way. We made beds and we emptied bed pans. We never made a decision on our own, and we obeyed doctors' orders to the letter. Other than actual patient care, we did little, and as part of our job, we had to make detailed and meticulous notes on every aspect of patient behavior and what we did to the patient.

This was true of almost every nurse who went into the Army in 1942. But in the Army, we learned how to be RNs plus.

World War II was the last hurrah for bedside nursing as we had known it. Many of the bedside duties of the RN were taken over by the LVN (Licensed Vocational Nurse) and the RNs became supervisors. Some RNs got college degrees and became supervisors. Now, most people going into nursing eventually try to get a Bachelor of Science in Nursing (BSN).

We learned to give blood transfusions, dress wounds, give injections, set up IVs and other numerous procedures that previously had been the province of the doctor. We were the vanguard of the contemporary nurse who does not spend the time we spent on learning bedside nursing while mopping floors and giving bed baths. Nursing, today, is more sophisticated and more technical. The Registered Nurse or the nurse with the BSN is a far cry from the woman who received "nurses' training" in 1940 and the years before that.

We had one male nurse in our unit, and he was not permitted to practice his calling. He was given an administrative job while the women did the actual nursing. In practice, he was in charge of medical supplies. Today, men are coming into nursing in great numbers and performing as nurses. And I must say that with the increased responsibility and professionalism, the pay has gotten better!

When I entered the next phase of my life, I continued to be active in nursing for quite awhile. I must say that even though we did not learn the high tech required of nurses today, we were thoroughly grounded in patient care. We learned the high tech out in the work world, but the training we got in bedside nursing has always helped us to be better nurses.

CHAPTER 8

Army Wife in Japan

WHEN I WAS an Army nurse in the South Pacific during the war, I wanted to go to Japan when the war was over. I spent two years in New Guinea and the Philippines, but never got to Japan. When the war ended, I was shipped home and mustered out of the Army.

Now, however, we were actually going to Japan. I was excited and looking forward to Ray's assignment to Yokohama.

In May 1948, Ray drove me and the baby right back to Smackover to stay with Mother and Papa until orders came for us to join him. Then he took the train for the West Coast and left for Yokohama by troop ship.

In Smackover, living with Mother and Papa were my sister, Betty Jo, her husband, Willie Bell, and their small daughter, Betty Ann. They were all in business together, running a supermarket and working hard to make it a success. They had pooled their savings to buy the business and were excited by its success.

My niece had what was called a "lazy eye." In other words, it was crossed. The eye specialist recommended that a patch be placed over the good eye to force her to use the lazy eye, but she was a difficult child—not well disciplined—and threw tantrums about the patch. It was decided that she would be taken to an eye surgeon in Shreveport for surgery to try to make the eye straight. Because I was a nurse, the family expected me to leave my six-month-old baby, Racky, and go with my sister and niece to Shreveport, Louisiana, for the surgery. I did, and we were there about a week. The operation was only partially successful, but it helped a little.

While I was in Smackover, I made some extra spending money by doing private duty in El Dorado. Not only could I use the money, but working also made the time pass more quickly.

At last, in late August 1948, orders came for me to proceed to the port in Seattle to join Ray in Yokohama. Papa drove me and the baby to Seattle, and then he flew back to Arkansas.

The trip to Yokohama took about ten days. This trip was quite different from the first time I crossed the Pacific. I got somewhat seasick, but my nine-month-old baby did not get sick once. He was crawling, and crawled so fast I was afraid I would lose him overboard, so I put a little dog leash on him.

I roomed with a nice Army wife and her little two-year -old girl. We got along well, and that helped make the journey pleasant.

When we arrived in Yokohama, Ray and other husbands were waiting at the pier for their wives and children. I held up our little boy for Ray to see. We were so happy to finally be together once again! When we tried to find the car, we discovered it was not on the ship with me. It was on a different ship, and that ship had been deployed to China to evacuate Americans. A civil war had broken out in China, and the Americans had to flee. I got the car about a month later, and, in the meantime, I had to ride a bus to the commissary. It was difficult because I had to load the groceries into a large cloth bag and carry it on my shoulders back to the bus.

Once we were settled into our home in Yokohama, Ray managed to get a jeep and drove us up into the mountains to Mt. Fuji and the beautiful Fujiyama Hotel. We stayed for a week and ate some of the best food I've ever had. They had goldfish ponds with the biggest goldfish I had ever seen in my life. At night, we hired a nurse to care for the baby so we could go downstairs and have dinner and dance to wonderful American music played by a Japanese orchestra.

Later in the week, the baby became fretful and began to cry. We discovered he had an ear infection, so we decided to return to Yokohama and the doctor. I wrapped the baby up well so he would not get cold in the open jeep. Back in Yokohama, the doctor at the dispensary gave him antibiotics and soon he was well again.

We lived in a small duplex in an area where other Americans lived. It was called Area "X." The small Tom Thumb type duplex had a small living room, dining room, and kitchen downstairs, and upstairs, two small bedrooms and a bath. It was not luxurious, but it was cozy, and Ray had worked hard getting it ready for me. He even had the pictures hanging on the walls. The only problem was we always had trouble with the radiators. At night, they would break, and in the morning the downstairs would be completely flooded! I had to put on rubber boots to walk around.

The wives in my husband's unit decided we should all take golf lessons at the Hodagaya Country Club. We took our lessons from Japanese professionals, and they were perfectionists. They would not let us go out on the green until we had absolutely perfected our swing. I thought I might enjoy the game, but I was pregnant and suffered a miscarriage. I believe all that swinging caused the miscarriage.

While I was in the hospital, I was worried about my baby who was left alone with the Japanese servants. At first, I noticed that he seemed afraid when he looked at them. I think it was because of their eyes. It scared him. I was told later by one of the maids that the houseboy actually abused him. He would swing him back and forth upside down by his feet.

Later, with the baby becoming accustomed to new servants, I went to work as a civil service nurse in the 155th station hospital. There I did shift work around the clock so when the opportunity arose, I transferred to the local dispensary where I worked 8:00 A.M. to 5:00 P.M., which was much better. Working as a civilian nurse enabled me to compare Army and civilian nursing. I found out when the schedules were made up, the civilian nurses got the worst shifts, but the work was easier. We did not have all those battle casualties. The equipment was better and more advanced. Also, now we had antibiotics. Nursing was easier and more modern. But we kept the responsibilities taken on during the war, and now we had even more responsibility. We started IVs, blood transfusions and changed dressings. This saved the doctors valuable time.

Another thing that was different was that we had more help on the wards. Young Japanese girls worked as aides, and we had plenty of corpsmen. I did a lot less bedside nursing than I did during the war. Now I was loaded down with paperwork —quite different from the days when we had no time for paperwork and got by with just a sheet of paper with orders.

Then we tended the wounded soldiers, and now we had to make entries every hour. Sometimes it seemed to me that some of it was a waste of valuable nursing time.

At this time, a lot of black marketing was going on. Lots of money was being made by those who did it. Sometimes we were shocked when some of the highest ranking American officers would get caught black marketing. Small time black marketing was done by some of the wives who sold coffee, sugar, and cigarettes to the Japanese. But the high ranking officers were dealing in really big time things like business machines and all sorts of things simple housewives couldn't get. Some of these people could take trips to Hong Kong and return with beautiful oriental rugs, expensive table cloths, china, etc. When they were caught and arrested, it was a big shock for all of us. It was hard for us to believe American colonels and Navy admirals would stoop so low as to steal, but they were arrested and put in the Army jail in Tokyo to wait for their trials. I would usually get their wives as patients. They were having nervous breakdowns and some had even attempted suicide. I couldn't figure out why they were so sick. They were enjoying the beautiful oriental rugs, china. etc. They were moaning, groaning, crying, and saying, "Oh, how could John have done something like this?"

All was not work, however; there was a lot of play. We had a busy social life—cocktail parties and dinners. Saturday night was dance night at the Bankers Club. The Japanese had a dance band and they were good. They played just like the big bands back in the States and had vocalists who sang American songs with Japanese accents. It was fun and we loved it. When the music stopped at midnight, we all started singing drinking songs until the lights went on and off, and finally we would be thrown out of the club.

I quit working when I found out I was pregnant again. At six months, I began to suffer from edema and started to develop hypertension and toxemia. I was hospitalized, and when an X-ray was taken, it revealed I was going to have twins! At seven months, the doctors decided they had to empty my uterus because I could not survive a nine-month pregnancy. Labor was induced, and I gave birth to a little boy and girl. We named them Daniel and Deborah. Daniel weighed a little less than four pounds and Deborah weighed three pounds. I had to leave them in the premature nursery until they gained five pounds. I brought Daniel home first. Deborah gained her weight slower.

At this time, Japan was filled with events. I not only had a miscarriage and gave birth to twins, but I also experienced an earthquake and typhoon. The earthquake occurred January 1, 1950, but was a small one. The house shook hard, but it was not a major disaster. On the other hand, we did have a terrible typhoon in November 1949. It was called Typhoon Kitty. From my New Guinea days, I remembered what hurricanes and typhoons were like and what to do to minimize damage. The other wives lacked the experience I had, and they did not prepare for the typhoon. But I could see it coming. Ray had to stay at his unit, and I was home with the two-year-old. As the winds got worse, brick shingles began to fly through the air at the speed of one hundred miles per hour. I had seen this happen with coconuts in New Guinea, but here in Japan debris was going through people's windows and flying around inside their houses. My servants got pillows and blankets and took me and the baby into the hallway so we were safe from flying shingles and other debris.

During the terrible storm, my next door neighbors came banging on my back door. They needed first aid and knew I was a nurse. The wife had gone to the window to watch the shingles fly through the air and had gotten hit in the mouth. Her teeth were broken, and she had glass in her hair, slivers in her face, and was generally a mess. When I asked, "Why in hell did you look out the window?," she said, "I just wanted to see what was happening."

I took care of her and later she went to the hospital. Her broken teeth had to be capped.

Ray came home about midnight and sent them home. Then he hung blankets in the windows. We took the baby into the bed between us and passed the night quietly. The blankets kept the shingles from flying through the windows.

When we had the earthquake in January 1950, I had already brought my twin son home from the hospital, but my daughter was still in the preemie nursery. I was scared when the earth and house shook. I wanted both of my new babies home with me. I went to the hospital and told the doctors and nurses that I wanted my baby. What if the earthquake had been very bad and my baby had been killed? The nurse said I had nothing to worry about because she already had my little daughter on the elevator and was going down to the first floor. Since the baby was very slow gaining weight, the doctor decided maybe tender loving care by the mother at home would help her gain faster. I took her home.

With both of my babies home from the hospital, I trained my first-class cook, Toshio, to wash and sterilize baby bottles, to make formulas, to squeeze fresh orange juice, and to put two drops of cod liver oil in each bottle for the babies. The houseboy, Nagasi, took care of our two-year-old son, Racky, and was given a lot of responsibility. He cleaned the house and did the laundry. All the maid, Toshiko, did was take care of the twins. When it was time for them to eat, Toshio assisted her. He brought the baby bottles and food into the room on a tray. Then he would sit and feed one baby while she sat and fed the other baby.

We ordered a twin stroller from the States, and Toshiko enjoyed packing the two little bundles into it and taking them for a stroll. Nagasi kept the two year old occupied, and Ray and I continued our normal lives.

Our normal lives included a lot of socializing. We played a lot of bridge. We played at night with our friends, Dot and Gus Peyer. Gus and I played as partners, and Ray and Dot were partners. If Gus and I lost to them, he would get so mad he would make Dot walk half the way home. He would get in the car and take off. She would be trotting behind the car, begging him to wait. He would stop and wait until she got close, then start rolling again. Finally, he let her get in and then they would go on home.

The wives in our unit played bridge once a month with the colonel's wife, Mae Handwork. Her husband had been a brigadier general during the war and later was kicked back to colonel. She never got over it. When we played with her, she always had to have coffee with cognac in it. As she played, she nodded, and would suddenly come to life and accuse everyone of peeking at her cards. I lived with it. I endured it. This was at a time when an Army wife did not dare cross the colonel's wife; it would be the kiss of death for her husband. Once a week, we had to meet with her at the Yokohama Yacht Club for a swim, bridge and lunch. We had to pay our own way for these outings. Once every two weeks, we had to go to her home where she had a Japanese man who taught us flower arranging. She felt we should not leave Japan until we could arrange flowers like the Japanese. We had to use our imaginations to make original arrangements, which she judged before we left her house that day. I never was very good at flower arranging, but I did learn what it was all about.

Our tour in Japan had its pleasant side. The scenery, landscaping, flowers and lakes were gorgeous. We went sightseeing from time to time, and the Big Buddha at Kamakura was one of the biggest things I had ever seen. Ray made home movies of me and two-year-old Racky standing beside it. We looked just like little midgets. We also visited the Mikimoto pearl farm where we could buy loose pearls and have jewelry made. They had the best pearls in the world. We could open a drawer and pick out the pearls we wanted. We also had a large PX in Yokohama. There we could buy beautiful china dinner sets, coffee and tea sets and cloisonné and pigeon blood vases. There was also a lot of ivory in the PX. Ray liked the Japanese ivory and bought several large Japanese figures carved out of it. When we returned to El Paso, one by one, the ivory pieces exploded from the heat. We never realized how much money we spent buying knickknacks until we had to fill out customs forms on the Army transport before we landed in Seattle.

We left Japan when the twins were six months old, and Racky was two and a half years old. We went home on an Army transport, and had a stateroom with four bunks and a large crib for the twins. Suddenly I found myself alone with three babies. For the past two years I had been used to first-class servants, and suddenly, I had three babies to care for. Because of the three small children, our activities were restricted. We could play bingo in the lounge in the mornings, and when we did, we took Racky with us and left the twins asleep in their crib. We did check on them frequently. We were not neglecting them. But one morning, the captain and his crew inspected the ship. Later we found our names on the bulletin board: Stateroom X—found two babies in a crib unattended. No one said anything. It was just posted on the bulletin board, but it was embarrassing, and we never did it again.

Racky was speaking English with a Japanese accent. When we went to dinner on the ship and sat at a table with some doctors and their wives, they were amused and enjoyed listening to Racky speak Japanese and English with his accent.

We landed in Seattle in July 1950.

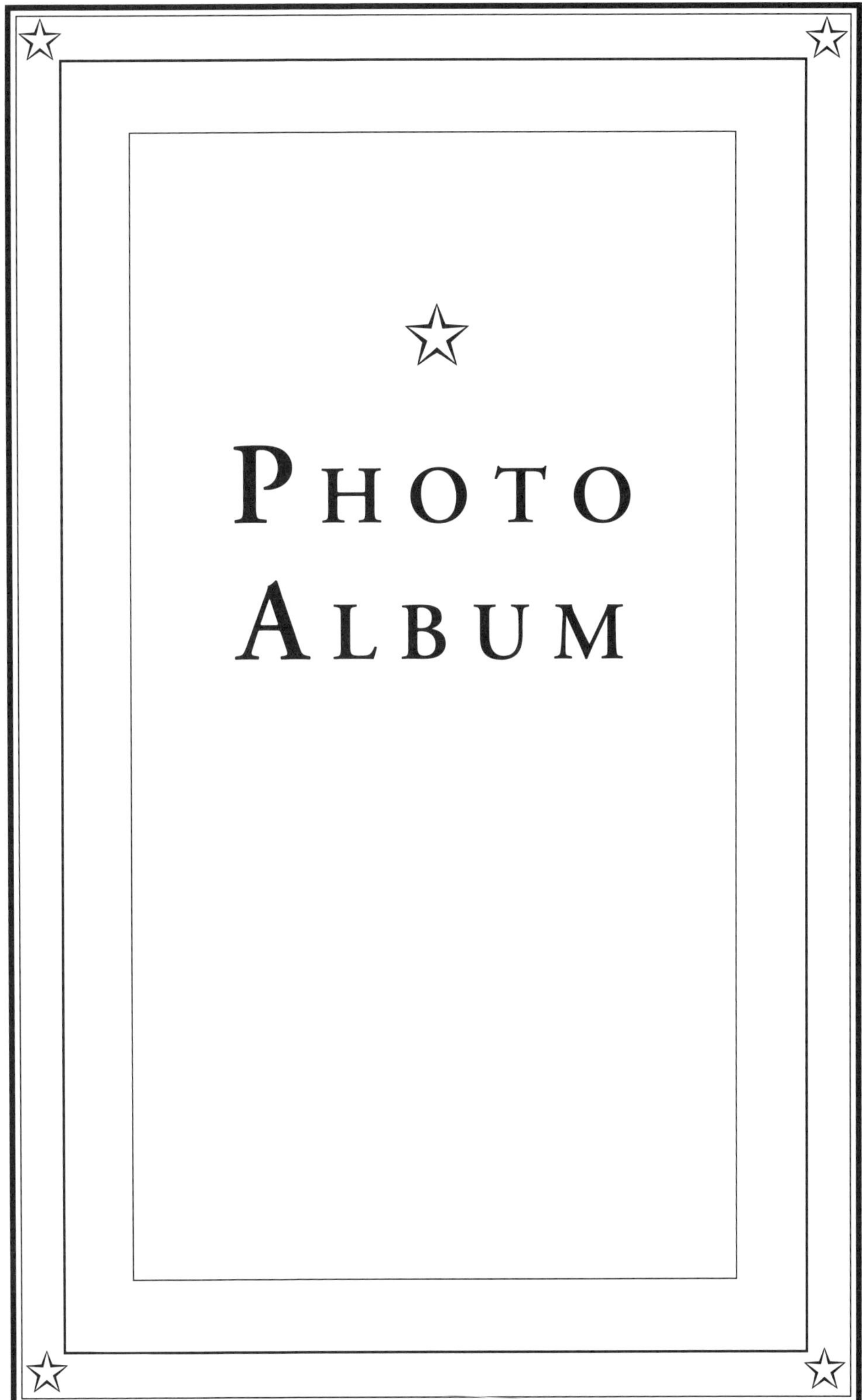

PHOTO ALBUM

Little Miss LaVada Bishop held by her biological father Charles Bishop at the age of 15 months, Arkansas, 1921.

LaVada with Dora "Big Mamma" Edwards, and sister Betty Jo in their riding britches, Arkansas, c. 1934.

High School
graduation from
Standard Umsted
High School
near Smackover,
Arkansas.
Class of '38.

Graduation from
Warner Brown
School of Nursing,
El Dorado, Arkansas,
September 1941.

The author, LaVada Bishop, after high school, Arkansas, 1938.

Mr. and Mrs. Raymond Aquilina on their wedding day in Leesville,
Louisiana, September 18, 1943.

Husband Ray in Germany, 1944, as platoon leader,
"B" Battery, 459th Anti-Aircraft Artillery (Automatic
Weapons) Battalion attached to the 29th Infantry
Division for the Normandy invasion of Omaha Beach.

First Lieutenant Ray conducting training on 40mm anti-aircraft guns on one of the firing ranges in England, 1944.

Rue's own private bath in a jungle stream in New Guinea, 1944.

Bathing in jungle stream, New Guinea, 1944.

Aside from bridge, most off-duty hours were spent sunbathing in camp.
Milne Bay, New Guinea, April 1944. The author with (TOP) Pauline
Martin, Kitty Clark and Peggy East; (BOTTOM) with Pauline Martin.

Summer, 1944, Lae, New Guinea. (TOP) Mary Adams behind the nurse's quarters in "the sunflower patch" alongside the plants grown from seed mailed from her folks. (BOTTOM) Prized watermelon grown by Hattie Hayes. She received the seeds from home and planted them in the fertile soil of the area—a veritable "feast" was had by all!

The author after the hurricane of April 1944, Milne Bay, New, Guinea.

Jack Benny with the U.S.O. Tour in Lae, New Guinea, 1944.

The author, Rue Aquilina, in Tacloban, Leyte, 1945.

U.S. fighter planes in Lae Harbor, 1944.

Japanese POWs in Luzon, the Phillipines, c. 1944.

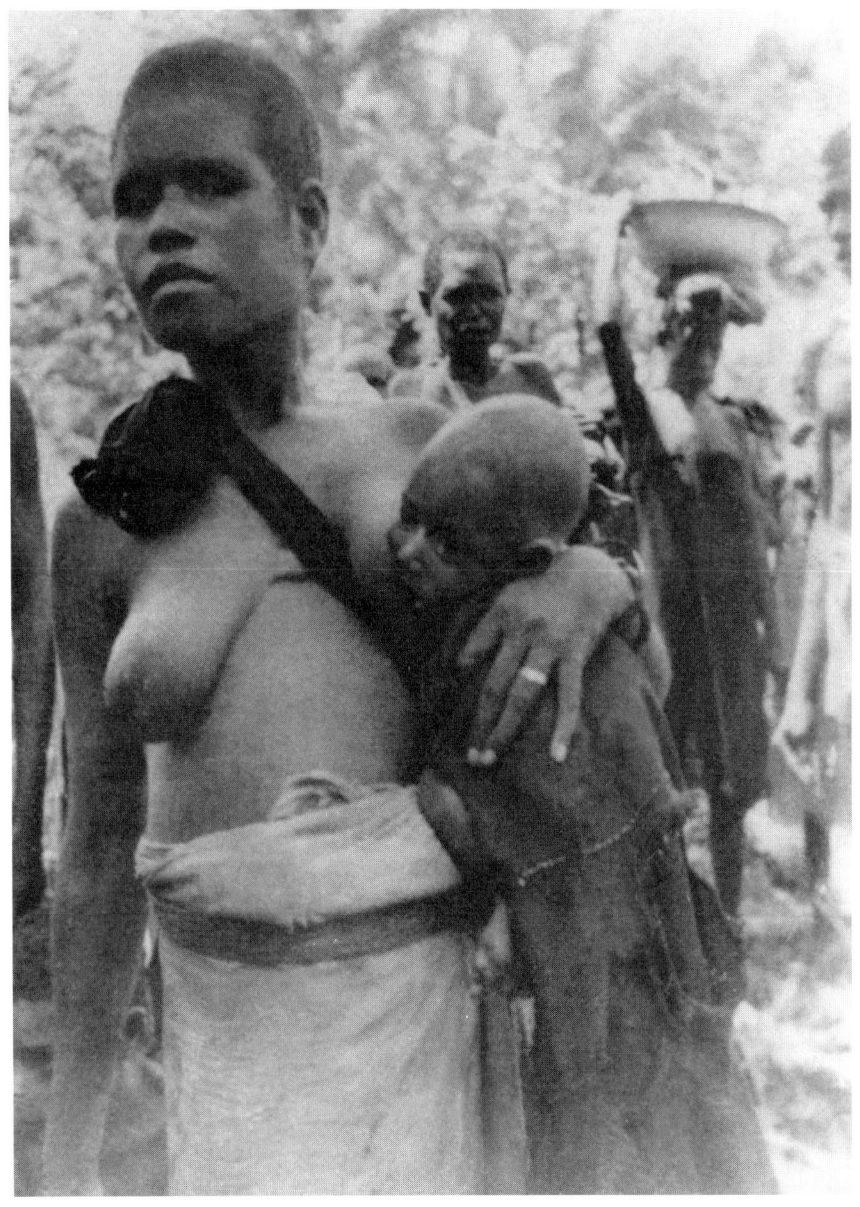

Native breast-feeding her infant, New Guinea, c. 1944.

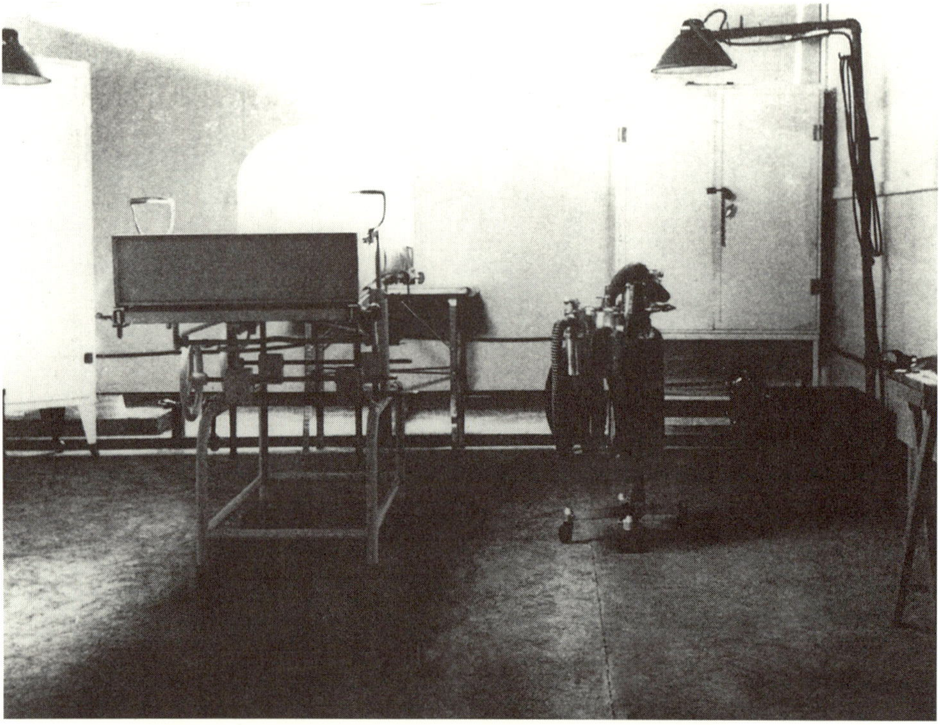

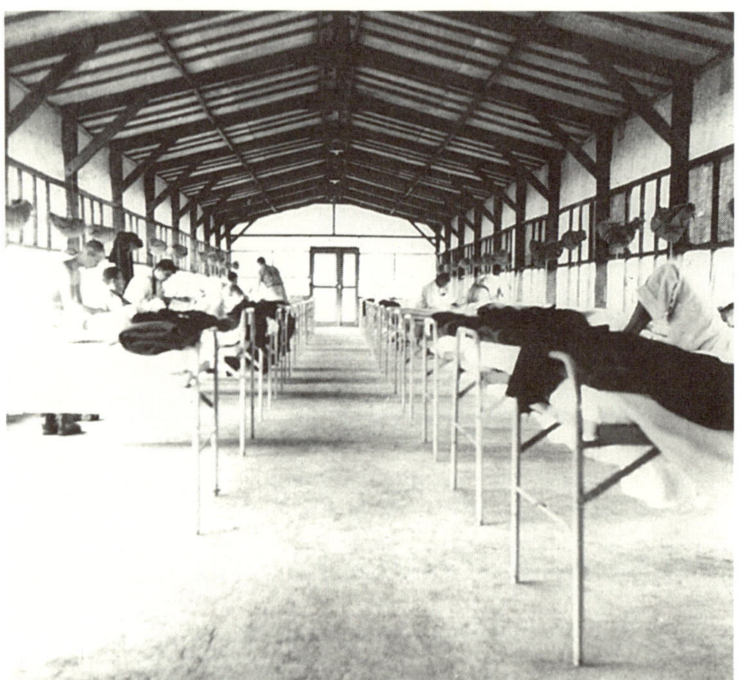

105th
General
Hospital,
Biak, 1944.
(TOP)
Operating
Room.
(BOTTOM)
Hospital
ward.

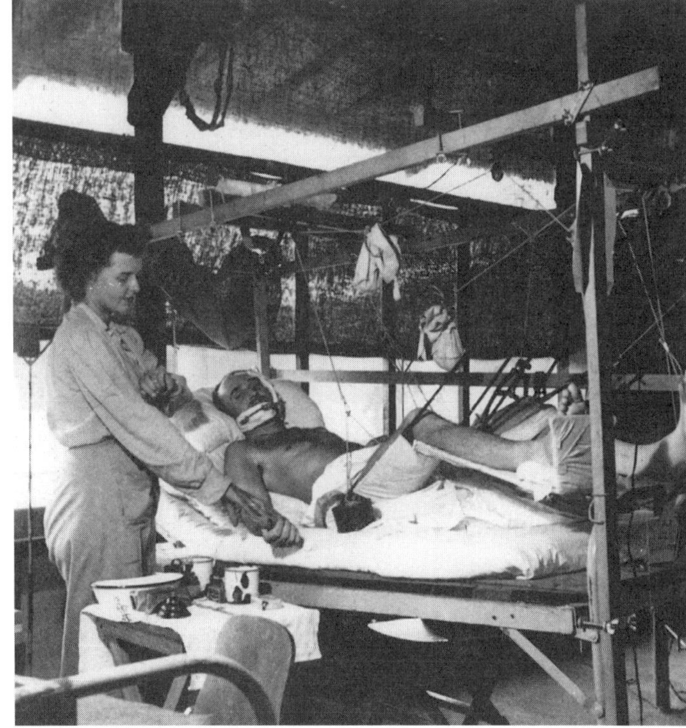

Biak, March 1944. (TOP) Maryon Peterson with patients at the 105th General Hospital (the Harvard Unit) (BOTTOM) Maryon Peterson with Orthopedic patient.

The author, LaVada "Rue" Aquilina, c. 1950.

Rue served as an Army nurse for five years but she worked a lifetime as
a civilian nurse in hospitals all over the world—a necessity in bearing the
cost of feeding five children since Ray's Army pay was not enough by itself.
She served as a civilian nurse at the U.S. Army 155th Station Hospital in
Yokohama, Japan while Ray served occupation duty with the 40th AAA
Brigade. At various stages in her career she worked at five hospitals in
El Paso, Texas: William Beaumont Army Medical Center, Southwestern
General Hospital, Hotel Dieu Hospital, Masonic Hospital, and the
Ft. Bliss Post Dispensary.

On board the SS Constitution en route to Athens, Greece, May 1967, the Aquilina family dines first class. Ray's three year tour of duty as Military Attaché to the U.S. Embassy in Greece began with this ten-day cruise which included stops along the way at Lisbon, Portugal; Gibralter; Palma de Majorca, Spain; and Naples, Italy. After landing in Naples, the family drove to Rome and then flew to Athens. Family members are (clockwise from left) Daniel, Timothy, Deborah, Ray, James "Rusty" and Rue. Missing from this picture is eldest son, Rack, who was attending the University of Arkansas in Fayetville.

(LEFT) Rue with her first generation of Aquilina children in El Paso, Texas, c. 1954. Pictured with their mom are twins Daniel and Deborah, born November 25, 1949, and first born son Raymond Jr. "Rack," born November 3, 1947.

At a Greek restaurant in Athens, c. Fall, 1967. On Ray's left is Greek Brigadier General Constantine "Dino" Papageorgio and his wife Alice, a dentist. Included are their friends, a Greek lawyer and his wife. By Christmas Dino had been imprisoned at the infamous jail on Bouboulinas Street as a result of a failed counter-coup attempt by the King to regain control of the government. Ray had helped get Dino and Alice's son, George, into Cornell University earlier that year.

While traveling in the north of Greece to Thessalonika Rue and Ray pose as the Greek and his wife, "Greek Style,"—the husband rides, the wife walks. c. 1968.

MAY 5, 1969

Party in the backyard of Aquilina house in suburban Athens.

(ABOVE, CLOCKWISE FROM LEFT) Rue, Mrs. Broumas, Lieutenant General Angelis (Chairman of the Greek Joint Chiefs of Staff), Ray, Professor Karahalios (Ray's Greek language instructor from the Defense Language Institute in Monterey California), Lieutenant General John Sorokos, Brigadier General Patakos (Vice President of Greece), and Lieutenant General Broumas.

(OPPOSITE PAGE) Lieutenant Colonel Joe Lepczk, Ray's Assistant Military Attaché is standing behind Rue. Also shown are Lucy Harwood and Air Force Major Bert Huskey. Joe was athletic and had played a lot of squash with the King. In addition, he also served as the King's karate instructor.

Rue and Ray Aquilina in Bangkok, 1993, during the year of their 50th wedding anniversary. Ever since Ray's "hardship" tour in Vietnam in which he had traveled to Hong Kong and Bangkok, Rue had always wanted to see these places, too. When they made the last of their four return visits to Greece they decided to also make it a "trip around the world."

The author, LaVada "Rue" Aquilina with Dottie Creech Ware, El Paso, Texas, Summer, 1995. On the celebration of the 50th Anniversary of the D-day Normandy invasion, the local newspaper, *El Paso Times*, ran a front page story, complete with color photos of Rue and Ray in their Army dress uniforms. El Pasoan and retired Air Force Colonel Bill Creech saw the article in the *Times* and upon inquiring with his sister, Dottie, now living in Newport News, Virginia, discovered that she and Rue had been tentmates throughout much of the war. On Dottie's very next trip to El Paso the two were reunited for the first time since the end of the war.

Fort Bliss and France

W HEN WE ARRIVED in Seattle in July 1950, we traveled by train to Smackover, Arkansas. The trip was as comfortable as it possibly could be with three babies. We reserved two rooms on the train and opened up the partition, thus making one big room so that all five of us could be in the same room. The twins went on the lower bunk and we used pillows to make walls for them. Two-and-a-half-year-old Racky was on a lower bunk, and Ray and I slept in the upper bunks. Everyone made the trip comfortably. A steward on the train made formula and sterilized baby bottles which he kept in the refrigerator until we needed them. Ray took Racky to the diner for breakfast, lunch, and dinner, and when they came back to stay with the babies, I went to eat—alone.

Ray had a thirty-day leave. We sold our car when we left Japan and now we had to buy another one. We bought a secondhand 1948 Plymouth. We planned to spend the thirty days resting right there in Smackover, but when Ray called his parents in Brooklyn, they insisted that we come to New York. I didn't want to visit his folks with three small children. They did not like small children and were very nervous when they had to be around them. But they wanted to see their son, so even though we couldn't afford the long trip, we went anyway. We put the three babies on a baby crib mattress in the back seat and drove off. Ray's foot was always heavy on the pedal, and we got speeding tickets going and coming.

At his parents' home in New York, the twins slept in a bassinet that Dorothy, Ray's sister, had put in the room, and Racky slept in the bed with Ray and me. Ray's mother had a washing machine in the basement, and I had lots of dirty diapers, but she wouldn't let me use the washer. I could take the diapers down and put them in the washer, and, later, she would go down and turn it on when she had time. Because she did not have a dryer, I had to hang all those diapers outside on a clothes line. At that time, there were Pampers, but we couldn't afford them. I had to be in the kitchen with her. While she was cooking, I was washing and sterilizing bottles and making formula, and I was in her way. She was annoyed because the baby bottles took up too much room in the refrigerator. In addition, she would not let me use her vacuum cleaner to clean our room. After two weeks, I was dying to leave!

The babies had not yet been baptized and that created an incident. Ray's family was very Catholic, so the first thing they did was take the babies to be baptized. Ray's sister and brother-in-law were godparents. Even the priest chewed Ray out for waiting so long to have them baptized.

After two weeks, Ray put the bags in the car, the babies in the back seat, and we headed back to Arkansas.

We got as far as Tennessee without a speeding ticket, but had a wreck. While driving on a two-lane highway, an old man in a pickup truck was ahead of us. Just as Ray pulled over into the left lane to pass him, the old man suddenly made a left hand turn without any warning. I had Racky in the front seat with me and grabbed his head as it went toward the dashboard. He was not hurt. Danny and Debby in the back seat were tossed into the air and buried in the bedding so deeply I couldn't find them. Then I heard sounds, like kittens crying. While I was hollering, "My babies! Where are my babies?," we found them and they were safe.

The front hood of our car was all bashed in. Ray jumped out of the car and ran to the pickup. The old man was climbing out. Ray yelled, "What's the matter with you! Don't you have an arm? Can't you signal??" This was before turn signals were put in cars. The old man was angry, and he looked at Ray and started waving a little nub of an arm. He didn't have an arm. He said, "I stuck it out!" But there was really no arm to stick out.

We had to call a wrecker to tow the car into the next small town. Because this was on a weekend, we had to wait until Monday to get the car repaired. We checked into the only hotel in town—it was inundated with fleas and cockroaches. There was no TV nor radio, so Ray and I played gin rummy. The next morning was Sunday. We went to breakfast at a small cafe next door and made plans to go to the picture show that afternoon. Ray said he would take Racky and go first, and when they came back to stay with the babies, I could go. After awhile, they came back and Ray was mad. They stood in front of the movie house and waited, but it stayed closed. Finally, he asked someone passing by when the movie would start, and he was told, "Don't you know this is Sunday? It is the Sabbath! There will be no show today!"

Monday came, and the mechanics worked on the car and had it fixed by Wednesday. We finally got back to Smackover.

As usual, the children and I were left there while Ray went on to Fort Sill, Oklahoma, for school. The first half of the course was at Fort Sill and the last half was at Fort Bliss. Ray wanted me and the children to stay in Smackover until he went to Fort Bliss. Here I was stuck back in Smackover. It seemed that no matter how hard I tried to leave, I always wound up back in Smackover.

In November, we finally got to El Paso. I didn't realize what a hard time I was going to have when we moved from Japan to El Paso. We moved into a rented house in Central El Paso. Racky had to grow up fast. He had to learn to dress himself and tie his shoes because I was busy taking care of two small babies. Ray was still a captain and money was short. It was necessary for me to return to work. I hired a young white girl from Smackover to take care of the babies, but it did not work out. She was too short-tempered. One day, I unexpectedly caught her screaming, yelling and calling the babies very bad names. She had to go! This was before the days of video cameras, and I was just lucky I came home unexpectedly and caught her in the act. I was sure she had been physically abusing them. They were not yet a year old and couldn't even walk yet. It was fortunate I discovered the bad situation and caught her before she actually hurt them. I sent her right back to Smackover.

Mother sent a black woman from Arkansas, but that did not work out either because she dipped snuff, and since the twins were beginning to crawl, I was afraid they would get into her spit can. I wound up hiring a Mexican woman. She did not have papers, but she turned out to be the most suitable. She could not speak English, and I worried about how Racky would be able to ask for water or whatever else he needed or wanted. I didn't have to worry at all. In no time, he was asking for *agua fria.*

We finally moved into quarters on post at Fort Bliss, and that was good. By this time, I had a Civil Service rating and worked 8:00 A.M. to 5:00 P.M. in the outpatient clinic on post. We started saving our money every month and finally had enough to make a small down payment on a small three-bedroom, one-bath house near where Bassett Center is now. Life in El Paso was uneventful.

Racky turned five and wanted to go to school, but public schools in El Paso could not take him until he was six. I managed to get him into Radford School for Girls. They took little boys in first and second grades as day students. Danny and Deborah didn't like this at all. They wanted to go to school too, and they yelled and screamed their displeasure at being left at home.

After a year, we sold our little house for a profit and bought a larger one in a location where a lot of military officers were living. Ray made a nice den out of the garage where we spent a lot of our time relaxing and watching TV.

In the summer of 1954, we were transferred to Fort Leavenworth, Kansas, where Ray attended Command and General Staff College for a year. By this time, Racky was seven and the twins were five. He was in second grade, and they started kindergarten. The twins were not happy about school, and sometimes I would find Danny had left school and returned home and was playing in the front yard. The twins had been born prematurely, and when I think back on it, I realize I probably tried to put them in school too early.

When his studies were completed, Ray got orders to go to France. He was fluent in French, and after VE Day in Europe, he attended the Sorbonne, studying French history and culture. He also had studied French for seven years in school. Now he was to be Liaison Officer to the French Field Artillery School in Chalons/sur/Marne, France. In August 1955, with our car and children, we sailed to Bremen, Germany. From Germany, we drove to Paris. There were no roadside facilities, and we had to stop and go to the bathroom in bushes along the roadside. We must have chosen a favorite spot because when we got back into the car, I smelled something bad and discovered it was on the bottom of one of my shoes!

I did not know it when we got to Paris, and nothing in my previous experience as an Army wife had prepared me, but France was to be a whole new experience for me. The experience was educational, but I cannot say that it was what I would have expected of *La Vie Parisienne.*

When we got to Paris, Ray checked into the Military Assistance and Advisory Group (MAAG). The first indication we had that this tour might not be very pleasant came during the first few days in Paris. We were staying at a nice hotel, and Danny lost control of his urine during the night. The maid reported it to the management, and we had to pay for the mattress. It was a small matter, but I thought it was somewhat unusual.

The next day, we drove to Chalons/sur/Marne where we met Ray's predecessor, Lt. Col. Bill Brand and his French wife, Yvonne. Bill had orders for the Armed Forces Staff College in Virginia, but was not due to start for three months. He requested and got an extension to stay in Chalons during that time and stayed in the house we expected to occupy. We had to move into a hotel. We needed two rooms. The rooms had bathtubs, sinks and bidets, but no toilets. The toilet was down the hall and around the corner on the outside. A good old fashioned outhouse! I was actually afraid my small children would fall in. One day after school, Danny accidentally locked himself in the outhouse. His brother, Racky, had to be lifted up and lowered through the space at the top of the door to unlock the door and to rescue him.

We took breakfast in our room. It was usually hot chocolate and the French version of toast. In the evening, we ate dinner at the French Officers' Mess. All of their meats were cooked rare and I couldn't stand it. I enjoyed the potage, vegetables, and fruits. The windows of the mess were not screened and flies and gnats and other insects got inside all the time. One evening, during dinner, I discovered what I thought were seasonings were really insects—some were dead and some were alive. I felt sick. As a result, we stayed away for a few days and ate in the local restaurants.

After three months of living in the hotel, the Brands finally left and we moved into the Villa Liege, Aulnay/sur/Marne, a small farming village. The population, including us, was about one hundred. We were about fifteen kilometers from Chalons/sur/Marne where Ray was to have his office as Liaison Officer to the French Field Artillery School.

The children and I couldn't speak a word of French. Ray was fluent in French and could read, write and speak just like a Frenchman. That is the reason he got this assignment. Now we were living in a small town where no one spoke any English, and the children and I couldn't speak French.

At first, we didn't know what to do about the children's schooling. Being the only Americans in the area and there being no American school posed a problem. Should I try to teach them at home? I was afraid it wouldn't work out because they were rowdy little things, and I was sure they wouldn't sit still and learn. The closest Americans were seventy miles away in Verdun. That is where we had to go to shop in the Commissary and Post Exchange, and that is where the nearest hospital was.

So, we decided to send them to schools in Chalons/sur/ Marne. They were day students at boarding schools. Ray took them to school in the mornings and picked them up in the afternoons on his way home. Debbie went to the Catholic school for girls named Notre Dame, established in 1488, before Columbus discovered America. Racky and Danny went to the St. Etienne Catholic School for boys, established a few years later than Notre Dame. Although they picked up the language rapidly, I could tell how frustrated they were at times. Racky had learned Japanese when he was little more than a baby, and now he was speaking French. In fact, when they had dreams, we could hear them mumbling in French. One benefit was that the children gained an international education. Many of their playmates in our village were Polish children who had escaped from Poland.

Although they had some problems with grammar, they became very fluent in French and did well in math. However, Racky had to use both languages in math. He would count in French, switch over to English, and go back to French— and often would become confused. He also learned that he could cuss his teachers out right in front of them—in English. All three had to learn English, history and geography when we returned to the States.

The children also missed their American customs. I remember that on Halloween, the children got dressed up in their costumes, and I made a Jack-o'-lantern out of a big, fresh pumpkin. They put it in their little red wagon and went from house to house saying, "Trick or Treat." This custom was not known to the French, but when we explained it to our neighbors, they played along and handed out treats.

There were matters other than language that disturbed me. At school, the children were given cider to drink for lunch. It was hard cider, like wine, and in the afternoons the children became sleepy. Also, they had to go to school six days a week—from 8:00 A.M. until 5:00 P.M. We could not go away on weekends because of this tradition. Discipline was also different. No one was allowed to talk in class and disobedience was punished severely. Once, for some transgression, Racky had to kneel on a triangular ruler for fifteen minutes and thought his knees would be cut from his legs! Another time he had to hold a heavy book in each hand with his arms extended, parallel to the floor. Remember, he was only eight years old!

Another problem was the bicycles. Each child had a bike, but I was in constant terror. Traffic on the road in our village was not regulated. Trucks and cars went at what I thought were outrageous speeds. Cars came screeching around the corners, barely missing the children, and then the drivers would cuss my children for being in the way!

Our house—Villa Liege—was large, with winding stairs and balconies off the bedrooms. It was cold. The furnace in the basement was too small to heat the house properly, no matter how much coal we bought, and we bought a lot. It cost $100 a ton. The hot water heater was also too small, and we all had to take a bath in the same water.

Aulnay/sur/Marne was a very small village. Most of the population of one hundred was rather distant and unfriendly. However, a few of the families were kind and friendly. There were no police, and there was only one telephone in the whole village. There was a town crier who rode through the village on a bicycle beating a drum to announce the news. All too often, the news was that the electricity would be turned off at 8:00 in the morning on Saturdays and Sundays. That meant we had to get up early to have breakfast before the cut-off time. No sleeping late on weekends.

The Marne River ran past our backyard. It was only fifteen feet from the back gate, and in the winter when the rains and snows came, the water ran over the banks of the river and would have covered our yard except for the six foot cement wall that surrounded our house. The bridge over it was the bridge that General George Patton and his troops crossed on his way through France. History or no history, that river worried me. I was always afraid my children would be caught in it, and one day I actually found the twins going out the back gate with their sleds. They were going sledding in the river!

To shop at the PX and Commissary meant a seventy mile trip—one way. However, there was a small American Petrol and Oil Depot about fifteen miles away, and we drove over there occasionally after supper to watch their American movies and to buy cokes. Ray taught the children to sing in harmony on these excursions. They learned all the American drinking songs!

I *had* to learn French. A French captain came to my home

once or twice a week to tutor me in conversational French. We were the only Americans there at that time. I hated going to dinners and receptions and just standing around and not understanding anything and not being able to join in the conversations. I felt stupid, so I learned enough French to have a simple conversation with people. I also learned how to play bridge in French.

Then I found out I was pregnant again. I didn't like the idea because the living conditions were so uncomfortable. I knew that things were worse when I was in New Guinea, but I was ten years younger then and had no children. Also, in New Guinea, I always had someone to talk to, but now I was alone in a country where I had no one to speak to and three children to care for and a fourth on the way.

When I was three months pregnant, Ray took us to Holland. It was during tulip season and the flowers were dazzling. He bought more than one hundred tulip bulbs, and when we returned home, he spent hours digging up the dirt in the front yard and planting them. We waited eagerly for spring and watched them grow. Suddenly, they bloomed all at once, and it was a sight to behold. One evening Ray came home from the office and called me out to the front yard to admire them. After dinner, he went back out to take another look. He came running back inside, gasping and yelling, and asked, "What in the hell happened to the tulips?" How did I know? I ran to the front yard, and, to my shock and dismay, there was nothing left of the whole bed of tulips but little nubs sticking out of the ground. Ray was so excited, running around and yelling, "Who stole my beautiful tulips?"

One of the neighbors told him that another neighbor was herding sheep down the street and our front gate was open.

The sheep ran into our yard and ate all the tulips. Ray did not say anything right away to the sheep herder. Every morning on the way to the office, he would nod and just say, "Good morning," and the neighbor would do the same thing. Ray kept thinking the neighbor would say something or at least apologize—but nothing. So one morning Ray said to him, "Did you know your sheep came into my yard and ate up all my beautiful tulips?" The old man replied, "Yes, but you left your gate open." That was the end of that incident. There was nothing we could do anyway.

Things changed when a young lady, Gemma Twig, who grew up in Brooklyn next door to Ray, came to spend the summer in Italy. Her husband had suddenly died of a heart attack at the young age of thirty. She decided to come to France to visit us for a month, and it was wonderful to have her there. I had someone with whom I could talk. There was not much to do, so she taught me how to cook in the Italian way.

While in France, I spent a lot of time at the typewriter, typing letters for Ray to send back to Washington, D.C. At that time, the French were fighting desperately in a place called Indochina and seemed to be losing that war. Our Polish maid, Irene, had a brother fighting in the French Army in Indochina. He came home once and visited with us. He told us it was a horrible no-win war. Ray was also sending reports on the French fighting in Algeria. I was young and preoccupied with my small children. I didn't know why the French were involved in these countries and must admit that I did not really care at that time. I was busy with my home and my general feelings of boredom. Added to these feelings were the dreadful things I was typing—reports about atrocities in

Algeria. Sometimes these reports went beyond the typewriter and reached into my personal reality. Occasionally, a band of Algerians would break through into France and completely annihilate a French village. When I heard about such things, I would think, What if they managed to get to our small village? We had no phone and no police. They could kill us all before anyone knew anything about it. I had gone through two years of actual warfare in the South Pacific. Perhaps it was because at that time I had no children to worry about that I did not feel the fear that gripped me now.

Then it was November 1956, and I was due on November 14. The first week in November, the French General Pinnochionni requested Ray to accompany him on a tour of some American military bases in Germany. How dare he! He knew I was due to deliver my baby any time. What would I do? It was seventy miles to the U.S. Military Hospital in Verdun where I planned to have the baby. I was mad! This was at a time when President DeGaulle was threatening to kick SHAPE (Supreme Headquarters Allied Powers Europe) out of France. I couldn't understand the French. Didn't we liberate them from the Germans during World War II?

Since Ray might not be with me at a time when I needed him, what could I do? I couldn't get in the car and drive seventy miles when I went into labor. What about my three small children? It was a dilemma. My doctor decided I would be admitted to the hospital in Verdun and boarded there while Ray was gone. Fine. But what about my children? They had to remain in Aulnay/sur/Marne with the French maid.

During the two weeks I was in the military hospital in Verdun, the underground in Budapest, Hungary, revolted against the Soviet occupation. The fighting was terrible, and

I was scared. The Soviets overran Budapest with their tanks, killing anyone in the way and cutting off water and food supplies. I was afraid they would run on through Germany and France. I had a small transistor radio in the hospital and could hear the Hungarians broadcasting with their underground radios, pleading and begging the United States to help them. At that time, Dwight Eisenhower was President. He and our government made no effort to help those poor people, so the Soviets put down the rebellion.

Ray returned from his trip with General Pinnochionni on November 12, and I gave birth to our son Timothy on the 13th. The water was not good in France, so the doctor said I would have to nurse baby Tim. Since I had not nursed my three other children, I was apprehensive and didn't think I could make milk. The doctor said if I drank beer like I drank Coca-Colas, I would make plenty of milk, so Ray went to the PX and bought a whole case of beer. I did not like beer. I could only drink a few swallows before starting to choke, but what I did manage to drink made plenty of milk, and I was able to successfully nurse the baby.

At that time, Ray and I had friends in Paris. The man worked for Sperry Engineers and was married to a beautiful Hungarian who had, at one time, been a movie star in Budapest. She had a small son, but was divorced from the father. When the Soviets overran Hungary, her family buried their silver, jewelry and other valuables in the back yard. Being a southerner from Arkansas, I was reminded of the stories of families who buried their treasures in their back yards when the Northern armies pushed south. The similarity stopped there. Because she was a theatrical person, the Soviets decided that she should convert to Communism. She was called in

and talked to, and when she refused, they gave her a little time
to think things over. When they called her in again, and again
she refused, she was arrested and jailed to think it over. After
a week, with very little food and no bath, she told them she
would convert, but first, asked if she could go home, take a
bath and see her small son who was living with her mother.
They allowed her to do that because they were sure she
wouldn't try to escape and leave her young son. However,
once out of jail, she didn't go home. She ran. For about two
weeks, she walked and ran through the woods and swam in
the rivers. She went without food, and finally reached the
border of Austria and freedom. When I asked why she left her
little boy, she said she felt she could do more for him from the
outside of Hungary. She ended up in Paris where she met an
American working for Sperry and they married. Then they
began efforts to bring her son out of Hungary. They hired
a lawyer who started proceedings through the American
Embassy in Paris to the American Embassy in Budapest for a
passport for the child. Every time they were close to bringing
him out, the Soviets would say his passport had expired,
and they would have to pay another five thousand dollars
to initiate another one.

There seemed to be no end to the delays. After several years,
they succeeded in getting her son to Paris. When they met
him at Orly Airport, he was a teenager. He was also deaf!
Because of his mother's escape from Budapest, he was denied
schooling and medical care, and when he developed a sore
throat and ear problems, he was neglected, thus causing the
loss of hearing. She and her husband started medical treatment for him, but there was psychological damage as well. For
example, whenever he spotted a policeman in the streets of

Paris, he would suddenly break away from his family and run. I never knew what eventually happened to the boy because, when I left France, I never heard from them again.

All this time, I was busy typing letters for Ray to send back to Washington. One letter warned of rumors that President Charles DeGaulle was going to kick SHAPE (Supreme Headquarters Allied Powers Europe) out of France. He succeeded in doing that, and SHAPE was moved to Brussels, Belgium.

One thing I never got used to was the hostility the French showed to the Americans. During World War II, the French apparently did not put up much of a fight against the Nazis, and the Germans thought that taking over France and Paris was a "piece of cake." The Americans who fought and died on June 6, 1944, were celebrated, and the liberating Americans were welcomed with open arms. But these people seemed to despise and detest Americans. I did not get on too well with the French. I was a registered nurse, and hygiene was important to me. The French standards of hygiene were not what I was used to. Neither were many of their other customs. Some of these differences were essentially trivial, but at the time, they were important to me.

I remember going to Paris when Ray had to report in to the JUSMAAG (Joint U.S. Military Assistance and Advisory Group). While he was doing his business, I window-shopped on the Champs Elysées. Then, I sat at a small table under an umbrella and ordered a ham sandwich and Coca-Cola. The soda was served in a small wine glass with no ice. The sandwich was delicious, but I remember wondering if the drink was kept in the cellar with the wine. This was one of the few pleasurable things I remember about France. I did enjoy sitting at the sidewalk cafe, sipping my warm coke, appreciating the delicious sandwich, and watching the world go by.

In Chalons/sur/Marne, we had to attend various functions. We were invited to balls and dinners and sometimes a combination of the two. Ray and I were usually separated at these affairs. He would be at one end of the table, and I would be on the opposite end. Protocol stipulated that at these affairs, husbands and wives would be separated at the tables. Even though my French was improving, it was still often shaky. When I fumbled for a word, I was just stuck—no one helped me out, and I missed Ray's support.

At the dinners, the first course was usually a dozen raw oysters on the half shell. I couldn't stand them. I like my oysters fried. But, in France, leaving just a morsel on your plate was considered a *faux pas*. We were constantly reminded of the days of starvation during World War II, so we were expected to clean our plates. Everything was served one at a time. First came the peas, and when they were eaten, the potatoes came, then the entree, which was usually rare roast beef, then the salad. After that came the dessert, which was followed by bread and cheese. Naturally, the appropriate wine—red or white—was served with each course and dessert was accompanied by champagne. I never did get used to it, and I am surprised that I did not return home looking like a stuffed and trussed turkey.

Besides all this, the weather was usually cold and uncomfortable. Even in the summer, we had to dress as if it were winter. The children and I wore long underwear, and when I had to dress for a formal party and take off my long underwear, I hated it. Occasionally there would be a warm day, and the children could put on their shorts and ride their bikes around in the village.

There were other annoyances. Once, after dinner, while we were in bed, the quiet of the house was disturbed by a noise in the kitchen. Ray thought I was imagining the noise, but I have keen hearing, and besides, there were no radios or TVs in the house. Ray would go downstairs, investigate and find nothing. This situation continued every few nights for two months. I could hear clinking noises, like someone washing dishes. Ray kept telling me I was just "hearing things." But one night it was so loud that even he heard it. We both slipped down the winding stairs, and when we reached the bottom, a large and furry thing came running from the kitchen door and actually ran over Ray's foot, headed for the laundry room and down into the basement. We discovered that a large field rat had bored his way through the cement basement wall from outside and was bumping into empty coke bottles at the top of the basement stairs, making the clinking sounds. Monsieur Liege, our landlord, quickly took care of the situation by filling up the hole.

Every Christmas we were there, we put up a big tree in the living room. I made candies and popcorn balls and bought stuffed Christmas stockings from the PX in Verdun. Then we had the town crier announce to all the people that children from ages one through twelve were invited to our villa on Christmas Eve for a party. We showed them cartoons of Mickey Mouse and Donald Duck on our Bell & Howell and served hot chocolate and passed out treats and gifts. Later, we read about it in the French newspaper. There was one problem the first year. The little children came into my house with muddy shoes, and after the party, we had a mess to clean up. The next year, we spread newspapers all over the floors to save work.

When Timothy was about two months old, Ray took us to Garmisch, Germany, where Americans went for rest and recreation. We stopped off at Weisbaden to visit old friends, Dot and Gus Peyer, and their daughter, Sharon. They had planned to go in convoy with us to Garmisch, but when we arrived there, Gus said he couldn't go, but was going to let Dot and Sharon go in the car with us. Three adults and five children, plus all the luggage, made for a crowded trip. A little trouble erupted when my children started complaining about Sharon pinching them. I resented that.

We finally made it to Garmisch, and we checked into a beautiful first-class hotel where most Americans stayed. I was able to hire a nurse to take care of the baby so I could join the family on some outings and sightseeing. We rented ski equipment and a teacher and tried to learn to ski. The children did fine, but the adults soon learned they weren't skiers, especially after falling all over the place.

We went back to Aulnay and continued our lives. Four months later, Ray received orders to go to Washington, D.C., for temporary duty for thirty days. I didn't know what to do. He had gone away before for one or two weeks, but I did not see how I could stand being in the small village of Aulnay alone with the small children for thirty days. As I have said before, in our small village we had no telephone, no police and no weapons. I was always afraid when he was away because someone would ring my gate bell precisely at 11:00 P.M., 1:00 A.M., and 4:00 A.M. At first I got up, went downstairs, and opened the door but found no one. I never did find out who was annoying me, but I didn't think I could put up with it for thirty days. I thought about taking the children to Germany, to Garmisch where there were Americans, but we really couldn't afford it. I suggested Ray arrange orders for me and the children to return with him and stay in Smackover while he finished his last year in France. He agreed, so we went home. After his thirty day TDY in Washington, D.C., he returned to France and moved into the French Officers' Quarters.

Now that he was living like a single man, he decided to go to college in the evenings. To do that, he had to drive the seventy miles to Verdun. He only had two years of college, and if he wanted to get promotions, he needed to get his degree. I thought it was good for him because it would keep him from being so lonely. There he could have some social life with other Americans.

Back in Smackover, I moved into the house with Mother and Papa. She loved having us there and enjoyed the children. I felt safe and secure there after two years of "iffy" living in France. I didn't miss it and the people I left behind.

The children were enrolled in the parochial school in El Dorado, and I went back to work after finding someone to take care of six-month-old Timothy. Every morning I got up early, fed the children, dressed them, drove them to school, and then went to the hospital to work. After work, I picked them up and we drove back to Smackover where they did homework. I took care of the baby, fed the children supper, and got ready for the next day. This was not exactly what I expected when I married and became an Army wife! But I have found out since that it has been the lot of many an Army wife.

After a long and lonely year, Ray returned from France, and we moved to Fort Meyer, Virginia, where he was assigned as adjutant of a brigade. We moved into a large white house on a missile site at Suitland, Maryland. The house had been

renovated for the Colonel and his wife, but they had decided
to live in Fort Meyer. That's how we got it.

By this time I was pregnant again. This would be number
five. I never thought I would have more than two children,
but it seemed like every time Ray and I had long separations
and got back together again, I ended up pregnant. Our son,
James Terence, was born at Andrews Air Force Base August
19, 1959. When he was six weeks old, Ray came home and
said we were moving up to Fort Mead, Maryland with the
Colonel who was being promoted to Brigadier General.
During this time, Ray was going to the University of
Maryland at night to finish his bachelor's degree, so I had
to make the move by myself with the five young children.

The movers came. Since I was nursing the baby, I had to
move from room to room to nurse him so that the movers
would not see me. Then Danny couldn't find his pet lizard.
The movers thought I was crazy when I asked them to keep
an eye out for the lizard. They never found it, and I had a
hard time getting Danny to leave without it.

We moved into a small four-bedroom, two-bath house at
Fort Mead. We had a large freezer, but there was no room for
it inside the house. It went into the small storage room located
on the front patio. I thought I would die! The door of the
freezer could only be opened part of the way—just enough
for us to slide things into it.

We finally got settled and the children started school. Ray
joined the general's staff as his adjutant, and continued going
to the University of Maryland in the evenings. Timothy, my
three year old, was not happy. He didn't like Fort Mead or the
small house. He cried and wanted to go back "home" to the
big house on the missile site in Suitland.

I went back to being an Army wife. I had to attend coffees, luncheons, teas, and took my turn being hostess for them. But in order to be able to do these things, I had to make arrangements for someone to take care of Timothy and James. I tried the post nursery, but Tim did not like it, so I didn't take them back there.

Some days I played bridge with the other wives. I found a very nice lady to come in to care for the babies, but one day she couldn't make it. The bridge ladies needed me, so they told me to come anyway and bring the children. They were both good babies, so were no problem.

This was my introduction to sherry. All the ladies drank wine and sherry and got happy. They laughed and talked a lot, and they seemed to know everything that went on in the brigade and told everything. That particular day, I drank some sherry and I was not used to it. When I got home, I was so drunk and tired, I put the baby in his crib, Timmy to bed for a nap, and I fell across the bed and went to sleep. The next thing I remembered was Ray shaking me, waking me up, and asking what we were going to have for supper. I hadn't even thought about it. Then he realized I was drunk and yelled at me and asked what I thought I was doing anyway! I was so groggy, I couldn't think straight. But I did know, though, that I would certainly be careful about sherry the next time. I also learned that those meek little ladies who said they didn't drink, but would take a small glass of sherry, knew what they were doing. They may have left the hard stuff to the men, but they knew sherry packed as big a wallop.

ALTHOUGH I was out of the Army, I continued my nursing career, and I combined my nursing career with the life of an Army wife. In addition, I had five children, and I can tell anyone that my life was busy.

I began my career as a typical Registered Nurse. I worked through the times that saw the traditional nurse give way to the more educated nurse who was an assistant to the physician. When I was in nursing school, one thing we learned was perfect penmanship. We had to learn how to print, and the nuns gave us lessons in printing. We were graded on the penmanship of our charts because the charts had to be letter perfect. From midnight until 7:00 A.M., we had to use red ink. We used plume pens that were dipped into the ink bottle, and if we messed up a chart and a blot appeared, we had to do the whole thing over.

When I was in nursing school, the nurses did the dirty work. We cleaned the utility rooms and did all the work that maids and orderlies do today. This was part of our training as students. We also focused on bedside care. That was the most important thing for a patient at that time. At 10:00 A.M., we passed a tray of refreshments to the patients that we had prepared ourselves in the diet kitchen. We made and served milk shakes, malted milks, fresh orange juice, lemonade, and tomato juice. Today, snacks come from a diet kitchen and are passed about by nurses aides and orderlies.

Obstetrical patients were handled quite differently then. Two weeks of bed rest was always ordered, and we had to give them the same care we gave medical and surgical patients. We gave bed baths and alcohol rubs three times a day.

Although we assisted the doctors when surgical dressings were changed, we were not allowed to do them ourselves. We just stood there and handed whatever was asked for. Only the doctors started the IVs and blood transfusions. However, we had to watch them, because the doctor did not always stay around. If a needle got out of the vein and started to infiltrate the area, we had to call the doctor, and he had to leave his office and come back to the hospital to restart the IV. Today, nurses start IVs and blood transfusions. I think the shortage of personnel in Army hospitals during the war made that change necessary.

We learned operating room techniques. In the six months we served in the operating room, we learned sterile techniques for surgery. We had to scrub our hands and arms up to the elbows for twenty minutes with a brush and sterile soap, then get ourselves gowned and gloved and set up the operating room for the surgeons. We were the instrument nurses; another doctor was the assistant.

On Saturdays, Sundays, and holidays, our duties were to make our own saline solution for IV use. We mixed it up and sterilized it in the autoclaves ourselves. We had to be especially careful because we knew that if we did not use a completely sterile technique, the patient might get an infection or severe reaction, and it would be traced back to us. We also made all of the supplies for the surgical trays that doctors used to change dressings. We made our own cotton balls and Q-tips, and we patched gloves to be reused for changing surgical dressings. In those days, nothing was thrown away, and very little, if anything, came prepackaged.

When I went into the Army, I did not know how to draw blood. I learned from doctors who were my patients. I also learned how to give IVs and blood transfusions. The shift in the area of my responsibility was, at times, almost overwhelming, but I learned, and so did all of the other nurses.

In civilian life, the doctors wanted the nurses to do as little as possible in the care of the patient. In the military, the doctors wanted the nurses to do as much as possible. The patient load would have been incredible in civilian life. The battlefields produced butchery every day, and every day the results of that butchery were delivered to Army hospitals. I believe that this was how the current path to nurse practitioners and physicians assistants began.

We practiced a simplified method of chart keeping. We were so busy that we did not have time to keep the complete, detailed charts of the civilian hospital. We had an admitting sheet with the names and ages of the patients, together with their addresses, diagnoses and blood types. The only records we kept were the narcotic records. If we wanted to know when the patient was given a narcotic, we just checked the narcotic book. Patient care came first; records succumbed to lack of time and lack of paper.

Penicillin and sulfa drugs were the only antibiotics we had at that time. Broad spectrum antibiotics came later. Actually, we were using some antibiotics in the Philippines, but a lot of patients died who could have been saved by the antibiotics that became plentiful later on. A patient with pneumonia was given oxygen, and it was administered in an oxygen tent, not nasally.

A lot has changed since I left nursing school. I am grateful to have been part of the change.

Another Separation

ONE DAY IN THE SUMMER of 1960, Ray came home from the office and announced that he had orders to go to Saigon. "What? I never heard of it! Where is it?" I asked if I could go and he said, "No. This is my hardship without my family."

I got out the encyclopedia and read up on Saigon. Indochina! Vietnam! I remembered my French maid's brother! I read that Saigon was the Paris of the Orient, and I wanted to go. I was told Saigon was not a good place for families. Some officers had their families with them, but they had to stay for two years and did not get credit for a hardship tour. Ray said he would like to go for his one year and get it over with. At that time—1960—there were only about sixty Americans there, and Ray would be one of a handful of U.S. Army Officers acting as advisers. He was perfect for the job because of his fluency in French. I was mad!

What would I do? Where would I live? We could not stay on post in the small Wherry house because we had to vacate to make room for another family. This was long before the

days of support groups for wives. We were on our own. I
know I was not the only one in this predicament, but some-
how or other, what was affecting me was hurting me then.
My life as an Army wife was not exactly what I thought it
would be like. It was getting harder and harder!

Ray wanted me to go back to Arkansas. I didn't want to.
I knew it would be another boring, dull routine of work and
taking care of the children alone, and besides, I didn't want to
move back into the house with Mother and Papa with five
children. It wouldn't be fair to any of us. I had been gone so
long, most people thought my sister was an only child. So
even though Smackover was a small town where everyone
knew everyone else, no one knew me any more. But that is
where I went in December 1960.

Our household goods were put into storage, and we stayed
with Mother and Papa until I found a house to rent. That was
difficult because Smackover was a small town and had very
few houses for rent. I finally found one with three small
bedrooms and one bath for which I paid $75.00 a month.
That was the housing allowance for a major at that time. It
was the dirtiest house I had ever laid my eyes on. It took me
and a crew of young black boys three weeks to clean it up.
The stove and refrigerator were absolutely the hardest things
to get clean I had ever tackled!

Finally we were able to move in. Since the pay for an
Army major was not very much at that time and it would
have to be split two ways, my part was not sufficient to live
comfortably and take care of five small children. I had to go
to work. I do not know what other wives did or how they
managed when left alone, especially those who never worked.
All I knew was that having five children to support and feed

and clothe, made it necessary for me to work.

I found a young black girl to work for me part of the day to take care of my two small children, Timothy and James. I got a job in El Dorado working in an emergency room. I chose the hours 3:00 P.M. to 11:00 P.M. so I could be home with the children most of the day and night. My little daughter, Deborah, would rush home from school to take care of the babies when the maid left. I trusted her completely, and do not know how I could have managed without her. She adored the babies and they loved her. She watched over them like a little mother.

Ray passed through on his way to California in February 1961. He decided to take the Volkswagen with him and leave me the old Chrysler station wagon. I wanted to get a new car before he left, but he wanted to wait until he returned. That old car gave me more trouble than any car I had before or have had since. Most of the time, I had to borrow Mother's Chevrolet station wagon.

My life was the dull, boring routine that I expected. No one in Smackover had ever heard of Saigon, and that was not surprising. I did not know of it myself until Ray got orders to go there. People looked at me strangely when I told them where Ray was. In fact, the people of Smackover thought we led a strange life, like gypsies. At school, the children had a hard time. Their accents were cosmopolitan, and it took them several months to pick up the slow southern drawl of their contemporaries.

I was not earning much money. The hospital administration decided that since I was a married woman with a husband to support me that I should (and did) get less than the unmarried women who had to support themselves. After I paid the rent and utilities, I did not have much left for food and extras. When December came, I worked a lot of double shifts to have enough money for presents.

We never had a pet, so I decided to get the children a small dog. Susie was trained to be a house dog, but if she got outside, she loved to chase cars. Sometimes I took her in the car with me, and when I went to get gas, she sat on my shoulders and would become a vicious little thing when the attendant stuck his hand inside to get paid. She slept on the foot of my bed, and if anyone came near the house, she would growl, bark and wake me up. We all loved Susie very much, and she was part of the family. One day, she accidentally got outside and was lying in the driveway of our neighbor. The neighbor got into her car and backed over Susie, smashing her to pieces. Tim was looking out the door and saw it happen. We grieved so much that I decided we would have no more pets.

Because I had no man around the house, some of the men in town let me know that if I was lonely, they would offer comfort. One tried to get me to go fishing with him. Some of the doctors even tried to date me. One actually wanted me to spend New Year's with him. He was stunned when I asked if I could bring the children. Doctors were among the most boring people I ever knew, and I never knew one who could dance.

Ray wrote often and sometimes he called on the radio-telephone link. He could speak, stop, and I could talk. It was not a very satisfactory way of communicating, and besides, his call was usually at 4:00 o'clock in the morning.

In Saigon, Ray was one of a handful of American advisers. He could not speak Vietnamese, but could communicate in French. One day, he and the senior advisor, Colonel Carl

Schooley, were sent on a mission to check the outlying villages for the Viet Cong. They were riding in a jeep driven by a South Vietnamese soldier when they hit a trap in the road. Someone had dug a hole across the road, and when the jeep ran across it, Ray and Schooley were thrown up and into the air and out of the jeep. They were quickly surrounded by the Viet Cong, but managed to escape into the jungle where they hid. The South Vietnamese soldiers slipped back through the jungle to get help and rescue them, but they were in danger all night. If they had been killed, there would have been twelve orphans and two young widows. Ray had five children and Schooley had seven.

Ray was promoted to Lieutenant Colonel in the summer of 1962. He decided to have a promotion party. I was disappointed. I thought he would wait, and we would celebrate it together when he returned home. But he had a cocktail party in the Brinks Hotel where he lived, followed by a dinner on a floating restaurant in the Bay of Saigon. He also had an orchestra. Ray always went first-class. He loved to dance, and there was no lack of partners. Some of the senior officers had their wives with them, and I am sure the wives got plenty of attention from all of the "summer husbands" whose wives were left behind in the States. In addition, there were Army nurses, Red Cross workers, beautiful slim Vietnamese girls with long straight black hair, as well as French girls and many Eurasians. He could dance all night long if he wanted to. I do not doubt that some of the "naughty" women were glad to dance with him and give him that old "pelvic ripple."

One day, I got a letter telling me he was going on an R&R—rest and recreation. He was going to Bangkok, India, and Hong Kong. In Bangkok, he bought me some beautiful gold jewelry; in India, he bought some brass tables with folding teak legs; in Hong Kong, he had some shirts and suits made. He offered to have some clothes made for me, but I said no. I wanted to buy my own clothes.

In February 1962, I received a message from Ray telling me he was being extended for six more months. The Berlin Wall was going up, and the Berlin airlift was started. Everyone was frozen in his or her job wherever they were. I was mad again! I was working hard to make a living and taking care of the children. I had no time off, and I thought maybe I, too, could use a little R&R—but couldn't afford it! It was about this time I seriously began to think about changing my lifestyle. I was actually considering a divorce! I planned to take the children and move to Shreveport, Louisiana, where I could study anesthesia and become a nurse anesthetist. I could make more money, and it was the only way I could support myself and the children and provide a better style of living for us. I was really fed up and tired of six people being cramped into that little house. It was not the lifestyle I had planned for myself.

About this time, my life eased a little. I was having trouble with the young black girl who was taking care of the children, and decided I had to replace her. I found an elderly black woman, Mary, who was divorced, had no children, and was tired of working in the cotton fields. She moved into my house. I put a cot in the laundry room for her. She was wonderful with the children.

Suddenly, in March 1962, before I had come to any decisions about what to do with my life, my only sister, Betty Jo, died of a ruptured cerebral aneurysm. She was in Little Rock, helping her eighteen-year-old daughter move into an apartment and get ready to attend the University of Arkansas at

Little Rock. I left my children in Smackover with Mary and rushed to Little Rock. I stayed by my sister's side for thirteen days and nights. Although the family hired private nurses around the clock, I was there all the time. I got so tired that when I stood up, I got dizzy. Finally, I put some newspapers on the bathroom floor and laid down occasionally for a short nap. My niece came in and out with her boyfriends, but she always spent the nights at her apartment.

When Betty Jo died, it seemed like the end of the world. She was my only sister, and we were very close. We were the best of friends, and she was the one who had helped me while I was alone and waiting for my husband to come home from Saigon.

My brother-in-law was devastated. He asked me to pick out the shroud, casket, and generally make the funeral arrangements. After the funeral, he asked me to choose a headstone for her grave. My mother tried to die. She practically lived at the cemetery, and it seemed to me that she forgot she had a living daughter. She lived with the dead. My niece never went to the cemetery. She said her mother was not there.

My children and I missed Betty Jo. She was good to the children and loved having them around. My oldest son, Racky, loved to go to her house and play pool with his friends in their rec room. He took my Waring blender there to make milk shakes for himself and his friends. I often went by at night after work and visited for thirty minutes. One night, I left my nurse's cape there. Another time, I let Betty Jo borrow my *Joy of Cooking* cookbook to get a special recipe. Ray had given the yellow hard-backed book to me when we were first married, and I had written a recipe in the back for little refrigerator rolls.

Two weeks after Betty Jo's death, my niece sent my children and me a message. We were no longer welcome in their home. We couldn't understand. What had we done? I wanted to be her best friend. She was my only niece, but she didn't want anything to do with me or my children.

Since I couldn't go to my sister's house anymore, I asked my brother-in-law to please return the things I had left there. He said he would try, but that was the end of it. I didn't get my things back. My mother was of no help either. I couldn't understand the strange behavior of my niece and brother-in-law, but then it dawned on me. I was the surviving daughter and stood to inherit from my mother, especially if Papa died first. Since Mother, Papa, Betty Jo and brother-in-law had been in business together for many years, the sudden death of my sister changed things. But I didn't want anything from them. All I wanted was to get out of Smackover, Arkansas.

Ray came back from Saigon in the summer of 1962. He had been gone a year and a half. Having a man around the house was strange for me and even more so for the children. James, the baby, especially resented him. He didn't even know him. He always thought the picture on the dresser was his father, and he didn't want the live version around.

We bought a new car. The Chrysler would hardly run, and when it did, it looked as if it was going down the highway sideways. We bought a new green nine-passenger Pontiac station wagon.

Ray had orders to command a battalion for the air defense of Massachusetts and northern Rhode Island, so we filled the Volkswagen with luggage and towed it behind the station wagon, filled the station wagon with five children and Mary and took off for the east coast.

Before reporting to the new station, we visited Ray's family in New York and stayed with his sister. Her house was not very large, and since Ray's parents also visited while we were there, they got the guest room. Ray and I—with Mary and the five children—slept on pallets on the floor in the basement, which had been converted into a rec room with bar.

All the aunts, uncles, cousins, and friends came over at night to celebrate and visit with Raymond and his family. Mary spent most of her time in the kitchen washing dishes while we danced, ate, and drank to music and laughter.

Ray's sister, Dorothy, had bad teeth, but had recently had them capped, and now she loved to smile and laugh. During the party, she overindulged in Manhattans, and then put on a floor show doing the cha-cha-cha all by herself. His brother, Rudy, came over alone because the family did not like his wife, Irene. They never did like her because she was bigger and taller than Rudy. Now she was a policewoman and packed a gun.

Uncle Jimmy Dalbora, Aunt Margaret's husband, owned a butcher shop in Brooklyn and had a bookie joint in back. Someone told me Uncle Jimmy had paid his dues in Sing Sing. Now, he was afflicted with narcolepsy and spent most of the time sleeping through the noisy parties.

Ray's father was an Italian immigrant who has passed through Ellis Island when he was eighteen years old. When he arrived, he couldn't speak one word of English, but he arrived just in time for World War I, and while serving in that war, learned some English. He had suffered a stroke and was paralyzed, so he was confined to a wheelchair. He was somewhat confused and cried when he should have laughed and laughed when he should have cried. He couldn't talk, but

Ray's mother said he told her to buy a mink stole for herself, and also said he wanted her to take him to Florida.

Finally, the family visit was over, and it was time to go on to Massachusetts. We arrived in Cohasset, a beautiful seacoast town. While we were looking for our house that had been leased for us by the Army, we rounded a corner down a hill on Jerusalem Road. The Atlantic Ocean loomed in front of us. Mary started screaming, "Lawdy mercy! Stop, Mr. Aquilina, stop!" She had never seen the ocean before, and she was sure we were heading right for the deep water.

As usual, the house was not big enough. We were eight people, and this was a three-bedroom, two-bath home. We made a bedroom for Debby in the dining room and put Mary in the den. That left the three bedrooms—one for Ray and me—and we put two boys in each of the other two. In September, we enrolled all of the children in school.

I became an Army wife again. Making the transition did not promise to be easy. For a year and a half, I had been alone in Arkansas with the children and working, working, working, with no social life at all.

The headquarters was located at Fort Banks on the other side of Boston. Ray and I had to drive there to make our official call on the commander of the brigade, General Frentzel and his wife. Ray's battalion was in Quincy, twenty miles south of Boston, and Cohasset was twenty miles south of Quincy.

The social activities began. I do not know how I could have carried out my obligations without Mary. As the wife of the battalion commander, I was supposed to set the example for all the other wives in the battalion—coffees, teas, luncheons, and cocktail parties and dinners at night. Ray's batteries were scattered all over Massachusetts, so Ray had to visit them by helicopter. The batteries being so scattered proved to be a real problem for young wives with babies and small children when they were expected to attend all of the social functions. The general's wife, who had only one teenage son, just didn't seem to understand their situations.

To shop in the Commissary, I had to drive down to Otis Air Force Base on Cape Cod. Sometimes during the winter, I would get caught in terrible snowstorms, and sometimes I was afraid I wouldn't make it back to Cohasset. I bought gallons of milk, bread, cigarettes, orange juice, and other staples. This was all stored in the big freezer in the basement. Everything went there that did not fit upstairs. This was my first experience with a "sump pump." Every time it rained, water backed up several feet into the basement, and we had to call the landlord to come in from Boston and pump out the water.

As had happened in the past, my children's accents gave them problems in school. Here in Cohasset, they spoke with southern accents and were teased and called "red necks." One day, Dan punched out one of the tormentors, and they were not bothered again.

In school, the boys were taking various courses in science and had to make reports on research they were required to do. Ray went to Boston University and brought back dog hearts, kidneys, livers, and cow eyes for them to do their research on. He put them in plastic bags in the freezer, and every time I opened the door, those big frozen cow eyes would be staring at me!

In the summer of 1963, Ray's year of command was almost over, and he had orders to report for duty at the Pentagon. He was being assigned to work in Research and Development.

When the children finished the last semester of school, we decided to visit Smackover before moving to Washington. Ray had to report to the Pentagon.

Mary and I and my five children and a friend of Racky's, Stuart Grimes, left for Arkansas in the nine-passenger station wagon. The first night, we reached northern Virginia and spent the night in a nice motel. The next day, after driving all day, we arrived in a suburb of Knoxville, Tennessee. I pulled into the Holiday Inn, and when the clerk saw me, he turned his back, so I had to get out of the car and go inside. He was cold and unfriendly and informed me there were no rooms available—no problem. I drove to the Ramada Inn and got the same treatment. When I complained that I had been driving all day and was tired and needed to rest for the night, the clerk told me he could take me and my children, but they would arrange for a place for Mary in the colored quarters. "That is not satisfactory," I said. I told him that I needed her to help me feed and bathe the children. Besides, I wouldn't think of having her separated from us because she would be terrified.

So, I kept driving and thinking. Perhaps we could cut up north to Kentucky and find a place. I had heard they were more accepting of black people there. I was driving slower and getting more tired all the time, and began to think we would have to sleep in the car, when suddenly I noticed a small independent motel. They were very understanding and agreed to put a roll-away bed in one of the rooms for Mary, and we all managed to get a good night's sleep.

The next day, we arrived in a small town south of Nashville. No motel would take us, so I drove to the police station and asked if I could park there while we slept in the car. I thought we would be safe there, but they said no way. So, I drove to a nearby gasoline station. We all went to the bathroom, washed ourselves, and I made the children comfortable in the back of the station wagon. Mary and I were in the front seat. She said she was not going to sleep. I said, "Good." I was completely exhausted and needed a little sleep. We locked the doors, cracked the windows, and since Mary didn't plan to sleep, I gave her my money to put in her pants, under her shirt. Then I slid down behind the steering wheel and fell asleep. Suddenly, I was awakened by loud snoring! Mary was sound asleep.

The next day, the children and I ate breakfast and took a tray out to the car to Mary because she was not allowed inside the cafe.

By the time we arrived in Memphis the next afternoon, I knew what to do. I stopped at the very edge of the parking lot and cautioned the children to stay in the car with Mary while I went inside. Several people were checking in, so I called to the clerk and asked him to come to the end of the counter. In a low voice, I told him I had a problem. I was traveling with my six children and my maid, and I needed two connecting rooms for the night. I was pleasantly surprised when the clerk said it was no problem. We could have the rooms, and if Mary was wearing her uniform, she could go to the dining room with me and help with the children. She was not in uniform, so we called for room service and ate in our rooms. After dinner, the children went swimming, and Mary stood at the edge of the pool to watch Timmy and James. If they got into any trouble, she was ready to jump into the pool to save them.

The next day we were in Smackover. Mary went to stay with her friends, and the older children went to the farm in

Prescott to visit Uncle Fred Edwards, Mother's brother. He took them fishing, horseback riding, and told them stories. He was a great story teller, and I remember the stories he told me and my sister when we were small.

While we were there, I had some uniforms made for Mary to wear on the ride back to Washington. Ray was there waiting. He bought a nice house in Fairfax, Virginia, and had it ready for our return. He was good at that sort of thing.

We found many of our old friends in the Washington, D.C., area. One was a lieutenant colonel and his wife, Bill and Prudie Lochrie. She was a nurse and worked in the operating room at the National Orthopedic Hospital in Arlington. She said they needed another nurse and asked me to join them. I had not planned to work there, but the cost of living was higher in Washington than in any other place we had ever lived. I knew it would not be easy, and I would much rather have stayed home to be with the children and be like a normal mother for a change. But it seems that if a woman is a nurse, she is expected to work, so I took the job.

It was hard. Mary got me up at 4:45 every morning and made breakfast while I got ready for work. Then I left for the forty-five minute drive into Arlington. She got Ray up and fed him, then fed the children and got them off to school.

My working enabled us to belong to the Officers' Club at Fort Belvoir and with reciprocity to Andrews Air Force Base, Fort Meyer, and all of the other clubs in the area except for the "fabulous" Army Navy Country Club. Dues for that club were $50.00 a month.

In Fairfax, we had a large back yard with lots of green grass and tall pine trees. On weekends, Ray and the boys worked in the yard, mowing the grass and raking the leaves. Sometimes I thought Ray was too hard on the boys. If they didn't follow his instructions to the "T," he would give them a hard back hand. Because I had been responsible for them by myself for long periods of time, I told him I didn't appreciate his roughness. I just didn't like it! I even called him "the great Santini." He was so meticulous. Sometimes, if he saw a leaf falling, he would run to catch it before it hit the ground.

While we were living there, President John F. Kennedy was gunned down in Dallas, Texas. We tried to drive to the Rotunda with Mary and the children to pay our respects, but found we couldn't get near the place, so we went back home and watched it on TV.

Life in Washington was hard for Ray and me. I was working hard in the operating room at the National Orthopedic Hospital, and sometimes Ray didn't get home from the Pentagon all night. He spent a lot of time on Research and Development for Robert McNamara, who was the Secretary of Defense. Ray did the work, but someone else was doing the briefing and getting the credit. Ray was well organized and smart, and the people he was working with knew it and used him. He was getting tired of it and looking for another job— away from the Pentagon!

One day in 1965, he came home from the Pentagon and said, "Honey, how would you like to go to Greece?" Greece! I had never even thought about that country, although I knew more about it than I had known about Saigon. He said it was time for a change, and he could go back to Vietnam and possibly get a star, or go to embassy duty in Athens as Army Attaché. My first reaction was, "But you don't speak Greek!"

I couldn't make up my mind at first. I had become used to living in Washington, and the children had made friends and were doing well in school. I liked the shopping and the culture of the area. Timmy had been a patient in Bethesda Naval Hospital, and they had done a wonderful job caring for him. Then I remembered Vietnam, and the incident when Ray and Colonel Carl Schooley were ambushed in a small village and could have been killed. I decided in favor of Greece. I didn't care about Ray getting a star, and besides, I was tired of all of the brouhaha of Army life. Maybe Greece would not be too bad after all.

Chapter 11

Attaché Duty in Greece

WE MADE THE DECISION to accept the appointment to Greece, but only after days and days of exhaustive self-examination. Almost every man who makes a career of the Army, consciously or unconsciously thinks about possibly ending his career with at least one star on his shoulder. When we came back from France, I was still young and naive and didn't realize that the stars came to certain people strictly through political channels.

When World War II was over and Ray decided to make the Army his career, I was all for it. I liked the idea of going to new places and meeting new people. We were both young and unencumbered. Now, we were no longer so young and we had five children. I had been left alone with the children, it seemed to me, too long and too often. The children needed a father, and I needed a husband and family all together.

Before we embarked on the Washington tour of duty, Ray had served a year and a half "hardship" tour in Vietnam. I was sure I was the one serving the hardship tour! While he was there, he had been ambushed and almost killed.

Traditionally, as a man made his way in his military career, the wife and children were not considered. That was as true for us as it was for everyone else. Things may have changed somewhat, but when World War II was over, Ray was a soldier, and the Army came first in everything. If he had to leave his family, he left his family. And in those days, there were no support groups. Each wife had to learn to live on her own and act as mother and father to the children. Some of us had to work to supplement the poor pay. I always had to vacate post quarters and find my own housing while he was gone. Usually, I went back to Arkansas—after having fought so hard to get out of there.

Communication between husband and wife, while the husband was gone, was almost impossible except by letters. The husband could call his wife on the radio-telephone link, but the wife had no quick way to reach her husband. A wife and mother of five children really needed to be able to reach her husband sometimes, and, all in all, this was not a satisfactory way to keep a marriage in good shape.

During our separations, I had occasions to cheat, but if the truth be told, I was so busy taking care of the children and holding down a job, I did not have the time or energy to accept any offers made to me. However, I knew several marriages that were broken because the wives were not strong enough and could not stand the loneliness. Husbands had the ideal opportunities to cheat, and I suspect they did. Some marriages broke up because of that too, but our marriage lasted. I was the one back home doing triple duty as mother, father, and breadwinner.

Then, when the husband returned and became the boss again, there often was trouble. The wife had become completely independent and did not need her husband to tell her how to run the household—she had been doing it alone for some time. That often caused trouble in a marriage. Even the children had to suddenly get used to having a man around the house barking orders and demanding obedience. God had come back home, and Mama sat in the back pew.

Many families who were separated had less than five children. Most of the wives did not have professions to follow, and when they were separated from their husbands, they did not work. Husbands knew they had to send enough money back home to take care of the wife and children. Therefore, they themselves had to pinch pennies. On the other hand, I had a profession, and that profession was in great demand. Hospitals never seemed to have enough nurses and, when they found out I was there, constantly hounded me to work for them. When I worked, it was easier for Ray. He had more money to socialize with wherever he was.

Some of the non-working wives even managed to join their husbands. Their presence was not officially approved, but it didn't matter to them. They got around it. With five small children, I could not even entertain the thought.

After a lot of thought and discussion, we made the decision to keep the family together and to accept the assignment to Greece. Ray forgot about a star. He still had his family, and he never regretted that decision. Because of his love of languages, I believe he actually relished the idea. He was gifted with the ability to learn languages, which was a talent many other Army officers lacked. He learned Greek rapidly.

Going to Greece was more than getting plane tickets and packing. It was more than putting furniture into storage and leaving our home. Getting ready to go to Greece took two years.

This was a diplomatic post, and we had to undergo a background scrutiny, the likes of which I had heard of, but never known. We had to furnish the State Department with the address of every single place we had lived since World War II, and we had lived in a lot of places. We had to list our children, where they were born, and when they were born. Our educational background was thoroughly investigated. Naturally, we had to list all of the organizations to which we had ever belonged to make sure none of them were subversive. We had to supply names and addresses of people who could vouch for our reputations. Our social and personal habits were checked out. How did we socialize? Did we drink to excess? Did we have attitudes that would interfere with the job Ray was going to do? Could we get along with people? They even looked under the carpet for all matters pertaining to our children—their habits, attitudes, etc. I got the impression that no one with a handicapped or problem child would be accepted for that assignment.

During this investigation, we continued with our normal life—at least as normal as it could be under the circumstances. During that year, Ray received orders to go to the Defense Language Institute in Monterey, California. We all moved to California and lived in quarters at Fort Ord. The children went to local schools. Ray started school in January 1966, but I did not start work until the summer when the twins were out of school. I had to wait because my two youngest children could not be alone. In the summer, the twins would be home and could watch the smaller children.

Racky was in college. He had graduated from high school in Fairfax, Virginia, and we decided to send him to the University of Arkansas in Fayetteville. That way he would have a base at my parents' home for holidays, but we planned to bring him to Athens at every possible opportunity.

I remembered the difficulty I had in France when I could not read signs or speak to people. I was determined that this time I would learn Greek. I wanted to drive my car in Greece and needed to be able to read the signs and wanted to be able to converse intelligently with people at the affairs we would be attending. Most importantly, I needed to be able to communicate with the servants.

After we completed language school, we went back to Washington, D.C., to attend attaché school. At this time, I remembered a book called *The Army Wife* by Nancy Shea. It was first published in 1941 by Harpers and Brothers. The book was written for the Army wife of fifty years ago, and I think it has been replaced by a newer book geared to the modern Army life. Our lives as Army wives were more re-stricted then than they are now. I think I was about the only working wife wherever we were stationed. But working or not working, I had to follow the Army rules of conduct for wives. Nancy Shea's book helped me do that. When I found out that I was going to Athens, I reached into the closet and dug out *The Army Wife.* Nancy Shea had a whole section on the con-duct of the wife of the military attaché in a foreign country, and I studied her as fervently as I studied at the language school and attaché school.

In France, when I was typing and doing other secretarial work for Ray, I found out that the Army often gets two work-ers for the price of one. I was not the first, and I am not the last wife who has helped her husband with his work. This aspect of my life was going to be emphasized more than ever as the wife of a military attaché.

The life of the spouse of a diplomat may seem glamorous, with rounds of parties and access to dazzling society, but the reality is that champagne and caviar are just the wrappings that camouflage the painstakingly hard and serious work required of the spouse. The military attaché in a foreign country is on duty twenty-four hours a day and so is his wife. He serves the ambassador, who is the personal representative of the President of the United States, and his wife is right beside him. Their conduct must be irreproachable at all times, as must be the conduct of the children. I learned that if a family stationed in Greece had a child who got in trouble, the whole family would be shipped back to the United States within twenty-four hours.

The wife of the attaché is expected to take an active interest in local projects. She volunteers at hospitals, is active in church, goes to all school openings and benefits, and does her bit for charitable organizations. In addition, she must cope with a steady stream of visitors. VIPs arrive constantly. It is not unusual for three or four congressmen to drop in for a few days—often on very short notice. Luncheons, dinners, tours, and receptions take precedence over the most important of plans. And the VIP thinks that this is a special treat for the family—a breath of home for those exiled in a strange land! If we did not know how to handle this graciously and with aplomb, we would not be diplomats.

And those little details make up life abroad. Nancy Shea suggested that I take with me two hundred personal visiting cards and two hundred joint cards, not to mention a good supply of engraved "informals" for simple tea invitations and notes. Life was going to be more formal than before. I was told to include many hats and gloves for luncheons and receptions and several formal evening gowns, at least one of which should be white. White was supposed to be worn when one was presented to royalty, but there was not much royalty left in Europe. But just in case we were to be presented, I also took a pair of long white gloves.

I also had to bone up on Greece. Nancy Shea said I should attend lectures and read up on Greece to become familiar with its history and customs. The first thing I had to learn was that I must never utter a single derogatory word or complaint about Greece. As a corollary, I had to learn to be prepared to have every movement and every word on my part carefully scrutinized and perhaps recorded and repeated.

Nancy Shea and her book helped me with my life as an Army wife, but her chapter on the life of the wife of the military attaché of an embassy was only the beginning of my instruction. The United States Government gave me a post graduate course.

In January 1967, Ray graduated from Greek language school. We took the children out of school, packed our household goods, and took off for Washington, D.C., to attend attaché school. On the way to Washington, we stopped in Smackover to visit my family and Racky and say our goodbyes. The trip from Smackover to Washington was without incident, although we did run into snowstorms that made the driving scary.

When we got to Washington, we enrolled the children in schools in Maryland. The life of an Army wife may be difficult, but I sometimes think it is impossible for the children. This was their fourth change of school in two years. I tried to assure them that things would be better once we got to Athens. Our posting was for three years, and three years in one place seemed a fantasy to our children.

With the children settled in school, Ray and I began attending attaché school at Ana Costa, Maryland. To gain entrance to the physical plant, we had to wear dog tags. Ray's dog tag was inscribed "crypto" and mine read "secret."

School itself was memorable. Our instructions and lectures were given by defense intelligence agents. Some of our instruction was given by Richard Helms, Chief of the Central Intelligence Agency, and his deputy, General Vernon Walters. Sitting in a large auditorium with about sixty other officers and their wives who were also heading for attaché duty, we learned things I never thought or dreamed about before. We were headed for all parts of the world: Iraq, Egypt, Iran, Jordan, Lebanon, Algeria, Bulgaria, Albania, Turkey, Pakistani, Japan—wherever we had an American Embassy.

We learned observation. We learned how to remember people by taking note of scars, birthmarks, moles, noses, ears, hair, eyes. We learned to listen to conversations—eavesdrop actually—and to take notes of anything we thought important. If we were at a dinner, whether an official or informal dinner, we were told to excuse ourselves and go to the bathroom to take notes. If we had nothing on which to write, we were to write on a matchbook cover or our thighs. We were expected to carry something with which to write at all times.

We learned not to have confidential conversations in our homes, cars, and bathrooms. The only safe places were beaches and open country, where microphones could not be concealed. We were taught how to look for and spot tiny microphones hidden in chandeliers, radiators, cars, or vases. We were, in short, given a first-class course in paranoia. Not only were we to be the eyes and ears of our government,

we were to record as much as possible. We were taught how
to use cameras to get revealing photos of strategic buildings,
bridges, hotels, signs, and shots of certain people in the back-
grounds. We even learned how to get into locked rooms and
buildings. I decided that I personally would never open windows or locked doors, but all of this material was interesting,
and I was taught how to do it.

The instructors not only instructed us in the need to
observe and record; but they also repeated much of what I
had learned from Nancy Shea. Correct protocol and correct
clothing were emphasized. Not only did we have to take a
white outfit in case we were presented to court, but we also
had to take one complete black outfit in case we had to go to
a funeral. I thought I would probably use the black outfit
more than the white one.

We were coached in the most precise details—even the
kinds of flowers to be sent on certain occasions. In some
countries, certain flowers are for funerals, others are for "thank
yous," and others are for romance. We had to know which
flower to send on which occasion in order to conform with
the customs of our particular station.

Both Nancy Shea and the instructors at the attaché school
advised me that although life would not always be smooth,
I was to make the best of it and never complain about the
country in any way. I was told we might meet with antiquated
plumbing that did not meet the standard we expected, that
maintenance men were often late in repairing fixtures and
plumbing, and that I must not lose patience with the
"mañana" attitude. Electrical surges might blow all electrical
appliances into oblivion. The open markets might prove
disturbing. The sight of meat hanging in the air surrounded

by flies might be an abomination to our sense of hygiene. We might come down with dysentery and need time to accustom ourselves to the food and water. Even when guests ignored the numerous ashtrays we placed about so conveniently and dropped their cigarette ashes on our best rugs, we were told to just smile. In short, we were not going to be in the United States, but we were representing the United States, and no matter how uncomfortable we felt, we were told to accept it all with a smile and graciousness that would reflect favorably on our country.

We learned that we would always be under observation. Every day was dress parade day. Not only would the residents of the country be looking at every little thing we did, but we would also be scrutinized by fellow Americans living abroad or traveling abroad. Perhaps if I had had a course like this before I went to France, it would have been a lot more enjoyable, and I would have probably stayed the whole three years.

In addition to going to school, we had other responsibilities. Ray went to the Greek Embassy and introduced himself to the Greek Attaché to the United States, Colonel John Sorokos. With him in Washington were his wife, Pia, his young son, Alexis, Pia's mother, Yia Yia, and their Greek maid. John was very popular in the diplomatic scene, and his activities were frequently written up in the social columns of the newspapers. We were invited one Sunday afternoon to their home in Chevy Chase, Maryland. When we drove up and were getting out of the car, John came out with his movie camera. Ray quietly said, "Smile, we're on Candid Camera." We also knew the film would get to Athens before we arrived there. Invitations to various diplomatic receptions were beginning to pour in. We met State Department people and diplomats from many other countries.

In March 1967, General Gregory Spandidakis, Chief of the National Defense General Staff of Greece, was invited to come to the United States on an official tour of some U.S. military bases and also some of the large cities in New York, Florida, and California. Since Ray was going to be the new military attaché in Athens, Defense Intelligence decided he should meet the general and be included in every event, including taking the trip. He was given $10,000 cash to use for expenses for the general, and we received a schedule of planned activities. Ray was scheduled to fly to New York City to be in the welcoming party at Kennedy Airport. The group would spend the night in New York City and attend a reception and dinner at the Greek Consulate in honor of General Spandidakis.

My instructions were to check into the Mayflower Hotel in Washington with a suitcase and whatever clothing I would need for quick changes. A Pentagon staff car with chauffeur was at my disposal and would drive me to the International Airport to be with the welcoming party. From there, we would take a quick trip to Arlington National Cemetery where flowers would be placed on the tomb of the Unknown Soldier. From there, we would go directly to Fort Meyer, Virginia, to attend a luncheon in honor of the general. That evening, there would be a cocktail party and dinner in his honor, and the next morning the party would leave for Florida. All of this was planned to take place over the Easter holidays. The night before the scheduled arrival, Ray received a phone call from Colonel Sorokos. The General's trip was cancelled! There had been a military overthrow of the Greek Government! Ray faced a problem immediately—what to do with the $10,000? He called the Pentagon, but it was Friday, and too late to return the money. He was told to sit on it until Monday. But what if we lost it?

Since it was Easter weekend, Ray decided we would go to New York to visit his family. We arrived at his sister's house with the children and the attaché case with the $10,000, which we stashed under the bed. We didn't say anything to anyone about it. During the entire weekend of partying and visiting, we nervously took turns looking under the bed. It did not get lost or stolen, and the first thing Monday morning, Ray returned the money to the Pentagon!

We took the children out of school early, packed, and were ready to go to Greece. We left Washington May first, and stayed with Ray's sister until it was time to board the ship. Two days before our departure date, Ray received a call from the Defense Intelligence Agency back in Washington asking if we would consider postponing our departure and return to Washington for six months? What?!?

Because of the military *coup d' etat* in Greece, the present U.S. Military Attaché, Oliver Marshall, talked to Ambassador Phillips Talbot and tried to convince him that he, Marshall, should be extended for at least six months. He seemed to think he was indispensable—that his knowledge of the situation was very important and felt like he couldn't be replaced. Ray thought the situation over and decided not to delay our departure. He realized that if Oliver Marshall could keep us from going to Greece for six months, he would have no problem delaying it for another six months. At that time, Marshall would retire. Obviously, if he was returned now, with only a year left before retiring, he would get some kind of minor or trivial job for his last year on active duty– which he was trying to avoid.

It didn't matter to Marshall that our household goods and car were at that very moment in route to Athens. We had taken the children out of school; we were packed; we were ready; we were going.

Defense Intelligence said to proceed as planned, and we did. We left New York on the beautiful cruise ship, the SS Constitution, for a ten-day cruise to Naples, Italy. We had suites on "A" deck and since we were traveling first class, our children were the only ones on our deck. At night, we had to dress formally for dinner. Before dinner, everyone gathered in the lounge for cocktails. Danny and Debby could go into the cocktail lounge with us. Timmy and James had to wait outside the lounge, but could look inside the glass doors and see us. After five days at sea, we arrived at Lisbon, Portugal. Everyone got off the ship and went sightseeing. We visited the beautiful botanical gardens and ate lunch at a seaside restaurant. Our next stop was Gibraltar. It was a free port and we enjoyed shopping. We really enjoyed our day in Palma Majorca, Spain. We rented a buggy and went sightseeing. While there, I bought some Majorcan pearls. The next day we visited Sardinia, and the tenth day we arrived at Naples where we debarked.

While we were sailing to Naples, we received news that there was trouble brewing in the Middle East. Many elderly people on the ship were going to Israel, Egypt, and other Mid-East countries, to visit relatives. They were told they would have to debark in Naples, or stay on the ship and return to New York because the ship couldn't finish its tour as planned.

When we debarked in Naples, there was an embassy limousine with a chauffeur waiting for us. The Army attaché in Rome, Colonel Ray Rafaelli, a good friend, had sent his chauffeur to pick us up and drive us to Rome. We stayed in a nice hotel near the Via Venetta. Rafaelli allowed us the use of the limousine and chauffeur during our two-day stay in Rome.

After two days, we boarded a plane for a short flight over to Athens.

When we got off the plane at the Athens Airport, we were met by a group of Greek Military Police with machine guns and escorted inside the airport. Waiting inside the airport were three people from the embassy—Wanda Lepczyk, wife of one of the assistant Army attachés, Joe Lepczyk, Jim Mack, a warrant officer from the attaché office, and Samos, chauffeur for the Army attaché. A huge bouquet of flowers was placed in my arms. I was already carrying enough anyway. Who needed to be bothered with flowers?

We wondered where Oliver Marshall and his wife, Eleanor, were. When we arrived at the American Embassy, they must have been watching from the lobby because as we drove up, they were at our car immediately, before we hardly had time to get out. Here we were, finally, in Athens, Psychico, where a large apartment had been leased for us temporarily. It was really a very nice apartment—more like a New York pent-house. There were four bedrooms, three bathrooms, large living room, dining room, small kitchen, and French doors that opened from the living room to a large balcony.

Eleanor Marshall put a piece of paper in my hands with a schedule on it. It had a list of names that I had to call on with cards. Mrs. Mildred Talbot, the Ambassador's wife, was the first name on the list.

As soon as our car arrived, I started driving. I wanted to be as independent as possible. In the beginning, the children and I spent most of our days at the beautiful Astir Beach at

Glyfada. It had an outdoor pavilion with dining room and live dance music. Some of the ships of our Sixth Fleet were docked at the Port of Piraeus, and the place was full of sailors in their swim suits getting drunk and dancing with young Greek girls in their bikinis—the "summer husbands" again!

Oliver Marshall managed to get his six month extension. They invited us to their home for an informal buffet supper with the children. The house was truly magnificent. We were told this would not be our house when they left. Robert McNamara, who was Secretary of Defense at that time, managed to mess up the attaché system. He divided it up and gave some countries to the Navy. Therefore, since Greece was surrounded by water, the Navy attaché was designated to be defense attaché. Captain Ted Davies was the naval attaché, and had already been there two years. He knew the Army house was the best one, and decided that when Marshall left, they would move into it. Colonel Bill Wade, the Air Force attaché, had been there before as assistant attaché, and, knowing the houses, said since he outranked Ray, he wanted the next best house, which was the Navy house. That left the Air Force attaché house for us.

After the musical chair dance for the attaché houses came the game of securing the diplomatic license tags for our cars. Anyone who knew anything about the embassies knew your standing in an embassy by the number on your license tag. Captain Ted Davies set out to take our diplomatic auto tag, but for some reason, it didn't work, and we kept the number eight on our CD tags.

During the summer of 1967, the Mideast war was going strong, and all of our diplomats and attachés had to be evacuated quickly from wherever they were—Egypt,

Jordan, Israel, Lebanon, Tunisia, etc. Half were sent to safe haven in Rome and half were sent to Athens.

The displaced persons who arrived in Athens were housed in the many hotels in and around the city. Their luggage arrived, but ended up at different hotels. Our Ambassador's wife, Mildred Talbot, called a meeting with her embassy wives, and we were given assignments. We were assigned to go to different hotels with a list of the displaced people and look for their luggage. All they managed to get out were themselves, their children and what luggage they managed to throw together. Most of them ran to their embassies. Many of the embassies were fired upon, and it was a frightening experience.

While I was matching the people and their luggage, I ran into old friends. We had lost them years before—Colonel Bill Kennedy and his wife, Tess. We were neighbors back at Fort Bliss, Texas, when Bill and Ray were captains. After a warm reunion, we invited them to our apartment in Psychico with their children for drinks and a good dinner. Bill was the U.S. Army attaché to Beirut.

A few days later, Ray came home from the embassy and said we had to have a reception for all of the displaced diplomats. It was in honor of General Vernon Walters who was coming to Athens to deal with the situation. Most were returned stateside for new assignments. Bill and Tess Kennedy were among those returned to the States because it was decided it was too danger-ous to send them back to Beirut.

When Ray said we had to host the reception, I was shocked because we did not yet have our household goods, so I had nothing to entertain with. Ray said we would have it catered, and the caterers would bring everything, including candles and flowers. All I had to do was be the hostess and greet the guests.

I figured I could manage that. I liked General Walters. He was most gracious and charming. I was honored to have the chance to host the reception in his honor. It gave him a chance to talk to the displaced diplomats and find out what happened to them and hear their experiences of how they managed to escape their terror.

Before we moved into our house, while we were still living in the apartment, we were instructed by our embassy to fly over to Cyprus to assess the situation there. Greece and Turkey were about to go to war in Cyprus. So we went on an investigative trip.

We were met at the airport in Nicosia by the American Army Attaché to Cyprus. He gave us a fast and wild ride through the city and to a place called Lemonaka where the American Ambassador had a cottage on the sea. There we had a business meeting, took a swim in the ocean, and returned to Nicosia for lunch at an excellent *taverna*. We lunched *al fresco* and the food was delicious. The flies thought so, too. I never saw so many in my life. They were teeming all around, and we had to fight them for the food. Above us, birds were tweeting in the trees, and we had to duck and dodge their droppings.

The rather lax hygiene, however, was the least of our worries. On the way to the cottage and on the drive back to the city, we had to stop at roadblocks, and I saw sandbags covering windows on houses and pill boxes on roofs and in the yards and patios.

That was my first introduction to the realities of our attaché life. Teas, luncheons, receptions and balls were only the outward trappings of the grim actuality of the reasons we were there.

But the social life did not stop. Finally, at the end of

September, Colonel Oliver Marshall and his wife, Eleanor, hosted a reception to introduce us to the Greeks and the diplomatic community. It was way past due. The reception was given in the garden in back of their house in Kifissia and several hundred people attended. We could not possibly learn all of their names in one night, but were given a list of all of the names and what their standing was in the community.

The Marshalls left Greece in December 1967, and the intervening months were not especially easy for us. However, we survived and I understand the Marshalls went to an assignment in Heidelberg, Germany.

Ray was now officially the Army attaché. I started to decorate the house for Christmas. We bought a large beautiful tree and trimmed it. We arranged to bring Racky over from the University of Arkansas for the holidays. I called Peter, our caterer, and made arrangements for a date to have a Christmas reception. Peter served almost all of the diplomats and no one planned an event of any sort without first checking with Peter.

Planning a reception for two or three hundred guests was a logistical nightmare. The first order of business was the invitation list and the menu. Peter came to the house to help me plan the menu. After this, I went to the Commissary and bought all of the food and stored it in the freezer and cabinets until the day of the party. Then the silver—all of it had to be polished, dishes had to be brought out, flowers had to be bought and arranged. I did not always have to buy flowers and never dreamed I would need so many vases. It seems that the invited guests sent flowers in advance. They arrived throughout the day. By evening, the house almost looked like a funeral home, but I loved them!

Peter, the caterer, came the morning of the party and

prepared the food. The kitchen had two stoves and they were both used to the utmost. These buffets demanded heavy appetites, and leftovers never presented a problem. Some women gained as much as fifty pounds doing their duty alongside their husbands. I am one of those people who never gain much weight, and I put on a little more than ten pounds during our tenure there.

No Army attaché could afford to entertain like this out of his own pocket. The State Department issued a generous allowance each month to help us promote U.S. policy abroad. Fortunately, I had my own china, silverware, and crystal, so I didn't have to go around borrowing from other people. Besides, they might be entertaining themselves and then where would you be?

In addition to large receptions, we also had official sit-down dinners at our home, sometimes for as many as thirty-six guests.

I had my first intimation of trouble in Greece while preparing for my first large reception. It was to be our Christmas party. December 13, 1967, I was shopping in the Commissary and ran into Jenny Bartlett, a Greek journalist for a Greek-American newspaper. She wrote the social column, and anyone who wanted her party written up in the paper always invited Jenny. She was married to a retired American Lieutenant Colonel, Roy Bartlett. He was in ill health and never went with her to any of the social affairs. They owned a home in the suburbs, but lived most of the time in an apartment in the Grand Bretagne Hotel in downtown Athens, across the street from the Parliament Building.

As I was gathering my groceries together, I heard some planes zooming in low over the roof of the Commissary. I noticed some of the Greek checkers leave their cash registers. Jenny came up to me and said, "Rue, something seems to be going on. I just heard the King is up north and has been arrested by the junta. I want you to call Ray at the embassy and find out what is going on." First, I went outside and asked my driver, Samos, if he knew what was happening. He said "No, but please hurry up and finish your shopping." I then went to a telephone and dialed the attaché's office at the embassy. The line was busy for fifteen minutes, but I finally got through. I asked Ray if he knew what was going on, and he didn't say much. He just told me to finish shopping and go home. I asked if I should go by the school and get the children, and he said to just go home. I told him I heard that "Maj" (our code name, short for his majesty, King Constantine) was up north and had been arrested. Then I said, "Jenny is here, and wants me to take her to her apartment at the Grand Bretagne." He said it was OK, and asked me to take a good look around the city to see if anything unusual was going on. At the Grand Bretagne, while Samos helped Jenny get her groceries inside the hotel, I scanned the area.

I saw machine gun nests going up on every outside balcony of the Parliament. Personnel carriers were racing around the streets so fast they knocked off the curb stones as they turned corners. And this was evidently just the beginning. On the ride back to Psychico, I saw many more personnel carriers speeding up and down the streets. I felt like something very serious was happening. Once we reached Psychico, I asked Samos to drive slowly by the Queen Mother Frederika's home which was on my route home. Two royal guards (*Evzones*) were always posted just outside her front gate, and they always stood at attention, never looking right or left, but straight ahead. Today, they were standing without their machine guns, and they turned their heads and looked at me. I believe they were looking at the American Embassy limousine. As I scanned the area, I realized the Greek military police had the entire block and the Queen's home surrounded. As I looked, two of the rough-looking military police pointed their cocked machine guns at me. I told Samos to step on it. We got home without further incident. After Samos unloaded the groceries, he brought our Telefunkin stereo upstairs. A small American Air Force base was located in the suburbs of Athens, and it had a small radio station that played music and gave hourly news. All Greek news was censored by the government. With the Telefunkin, I could pick up BBC. This could not fall under Greek censorship. We could always get in detail what was going on through BBC.

I found out King Constantine and the royal family flew north to Salonika the morning of December 13, 1967. When they left for Salonika, they had their pets, nursemaids, the Queen's obstetrician (she was pregnant), the Queen Mother, his younger sister, Irene, dozens of trunks, two airplanes, and Prime Minister Kollias, who was defecting to the King's side.

The King's pitiable coup effort took just a few hours to fail. The royalist side controlled the regular Salonika radio for only a couple of hours, during which the message was broadcast to the generals in the north who were to support the effort. Then the junta took possession of the radio. Constantine sent one of his generals to the Greek Pentagon with a letter to General Angelis, Chief of the Armed Forces under the junta, relieving him of his command and appointing the bearer of the message to succeed him. Angelis put the royalist general in jail as soon as he read the letter. The Papadopoulos agents arrested the senior officers who had proven in the most blatant way their disloyalty to the junta. In this manner, Papadopoulos was able, through the instrument of the King's abortive counter-coup, to identify and jail the remaining royalist supporters in the upper echelons of the Hellenic Armed Services. They were the most dedicated pro-NATO members of the Greek officer corps and had the closest contact with the Americans. The corps was now thoroughly decimated. The King and his enormous personal retinue fled to Italy. I remember listening to BBC when he was winging in over Italy requesting to land there for safe haven.

Efforts by the embassy to find out what was going on were complicated by the fact that the American Consul-General was off hunting in Yugoslavia and his deputy had driven to Athens to buy liquor from the Commissary for his own and his colleagues' larders.

The King was extremely disappointed because he had the impression that the United States would not remain indifferent, and there would be a showing of American interest.

Papadopoulos sent Ambassador Phillips Talbot a message that he wanted to see him. He wanted to know what Talbot knew about the King's schemes. Whose side was the American ambassador on?

From that moment on, Talbot's usefulness as the American Ambassador to Greece was all but finished. The junta never trusted him again. Later, the junta found discarded letters of support for the King from civilian leaders such as Karamanlis and Papandreou.

CHAPTER 12

After the Abortive Counter-Coup

I LOOK BACK on December 13, 1967 and see it as a perfect example of how the superficial aspects of foreign relations are carried on while the most profound aspects of these relations (war, revolution, death) proceed simultaneously. I was preparing for my first big formal reception and the country was in a state of revolution! But the preparations continued, and I stewed alone, wondering what to do next until Ray came home from the embassy with a new list of invitees. Half of my original guest list was now in jail or had fled the country. This list contained the names and jobs of all the new Chiefs of the Greek Armed Forces. Ray was supposed to stay close to everyone. I think he was expected to develop psychic powers and read their minds. But what that meant was that life went on. Parties and receptions continued; only the guest lists were revised. And I had my Christmas party! A relatively bloodless revolution could not stop the wheels of diplomacy.

As for the King, he and his retinue fled to Italy. He thought December 13 would be lucky, but he was wrong. The consequences for the United States Embassy were severe. The

American Ambassador was now a cripple, and although he remained at his post for another year, he was merely a figurehead. No one in the Greek military regime trusted him. This abortive counter-coup occurred nine months after the coup of April 21, 1967. At that time, the colonels took command of the country and Constantine went along with it. Things were peaceful for awhile until December 13, when the King tried to get his country back.

Since Joe and Wanda Lepczyk had been in Athens four years, they knew everyone. They proved to be invaluable to Ray. They gave a dinner in their home and introduced us to some of the key military officers of the current regime.

They had a life-size nude painting of a very ugly blond woman hanging over the fireplace in their living room. I loved to watch the Greek officers when they first noticed it. They were shocked and quickly looked away. Then, when they thought no one was looking at them, they casually took a closer look. At this dinner, we met a Greek brigadier general, Constantine Papageorgiou and his wife, Aliki (Alice), who was a practicing dentist. He was called Dinos, and was the commander of all Greek troops surrounding Athens. They had one son, George, who became a friend of our twins, Danny and Debby. Alice nagged me because Debby did not call George, and I told her that in the United States the boys usually called the girls. For all I knew, it was that way in Greece, too.

When George graduated from high school the summer of 1968, Dinos and Alice decided to send him to the United States to go to college. They asked for our help in selecting a school. They wanted not just any ordinary university like the University of Arkansas or Texas—they wanted Ivy League. That was the Greek way. They decided on Cornell, and we helped to arrange for George to go there.

We developed a close relationship with Alice and Dinos. He told us all about the civil war in Greece against the communists during the 1940s. There was a lot of fierce fighting, especially in the mountains in northern Greece. Dinos told us he was the only survivor of a family of eight. His entire family was executed by the communists during the civil war. Dinos was the only one left in his family, and he was a hunted man. His military friends helped hide him until the hostilities were over.

When we met him, he was in a quandary. He was torn between his loyalty to the military dictatorship and to the royalists who were committed to King Constantine. Remember, Dinos' first name was Constantine.

The junta trusted no one, and both civilians and military were under constant surveillance.

At all of the diplomatic dinners and receptions, there were whispers and quiet talk about the military regime in Greece. I was curious because living in a country under military rule was new and strange for me. I didn't feel very comfortable and never knew what to expect. I heard rumors of arrests and tortures. We were socializing with the rulers of Greece practically every night, and when I asked a key general's wife questions, she would simply reply, "My dear, my husband is a soldier—he just follows orders."

From 1962 until 1967 there were eleven changes of government by decree or coup.

I wondered what happened that night of April 21, 1967. I found out that about 5:00 o'clock on the morning of April 21, the key people with the American Embassy were caught off guard when they were awakened with the news that the military controlled Athens. All communications had been cut and all movement on the streets forbidden. Combat-equipped troops controlled every radio transmitter, airport, railway station, telephone central, power plant, police station and intersection. The revolution of April 21 was staged by a group of military intelligence officers headed by Colonel George Papadopoulos. The takeover followed the lines of a NATO contingency plan, code-named "Prometheus," designed to impose internal order and eliminate "subversive" leftist opposition in the event of a war with any of Greece's neighbors to the north: Bulgaria, Albania, or Yugoslavia.

The Greek intelligence agency, known by the acronym KYP, was established under the direction of the CIA, and the personnel and functions of the two intelligence bureaucracies were closely intermingled.

The royal family was an important client of the American CIA. Queen Frederika and King Paul, as well as the Crown Prince and later King Constantine, maintained warm personal relations with top CIA officials. Frederika was a woman of scathing bluntness and once remarked in the presence of a high-ranking U.S. intelligence official: "The diplomats are fairies and half-wits." She preferred doing her business through the CIA station in Athens. She was the recipient of many gifts from the agency, and one of the American ambassadors to Greece complained to Washington about the continued practice of playing Santa Claus to the palace.

By September 1967, we had moved into our house in Psychico, and the children were getting enrolled in school at the American Academy in Halandri. The house was much nicer than we expected. On the first floor there was a large foyer and winding stairs leading up to four bedrooms and two bathrooms. At the top of the stairs was a large open space where Ray had his desk. Downstairs was a large living room, dining room, bathroom, and a kitchen with a marble sink. All of the bathrooms had sinks, toilets, and bathtubs made of marble. I was living in marble halls! In the basement there was a laundry room, bath with shower and toilet, and four bedrooms. There was plenty of room for our large freezer. There was also a rec room with TV and stereo for the children. There was a garage in the basement, but the door was too small for American cars, so our private car and the embassy limousine both had to be kept on the street in front of the house. Out back there was a large sunken marble patio with a blue awning over it. That is where we had most of our receptions nine months out of the year.

There were two assistant Army attachés. One was Lieutenant Colonel Joe Lepczyk and the other was Lieutenant Colonel Ralph Karst. Joe had been there for about four years. He was there at the request of young King Constantine. Constantine had visited the United States when he was a young prince, and Joe was his escort officer. Constantine was an enthusiastic sportsman and Joe was an athlete. He had a black belt in karate and judo, and played tennis and squash. The King liked that, and when he became King, he went to the American Embassy and requested that Joe be sent to Greece for embassy duty. So, Joe was assistant Army attaché, but was at the beck and call of the King at all times. He was a national asset for the United States.

In the summertime, young King Juan Carlos of Spain visited Athens with his wife, Queen Sophia, sister of Constantine. They usually spent the summer in Greece visiting the royal family. During that time, Joe was at their beck and call, playing all of the sports the young kings liked.

George and Andreas Papandreou

T HE PAPANDREOUS, George and Andreas, father and son, were parties to changing political attitudes during the early 1960s. They leaned to the left, and their policies were regarded as anti-military, anti-royalist, anti-NATO, and even anti-American. George was a former prime minister, and it seemed the people of Greece loved him, but not his son, Andreas. Andreas had become involved in left-wing politics as a young man and had been arrested and possibly tortured when the Metaxas dictatorship discovered some of his political activity. His father sent him to the United Sates where he spent twenty years studying at Harvard and then teaching at universities in the Midwest and Berkeley, California. He met and married Margaret, who came from a small town in Illinois, and they had four children. Andreas became an American citizen and did a stint in the United States Navy.

When he returned to Greece in 1959, he delved into politics. In 1967, he was running for prime minister. My Greek friends told me he was disrupting the government by leading demonstrations and strikes. Andreas was suspicious that his telephones and those of his father were being tapped by the KYP and/or the CIA, and finally set up his own intelligence service and placed some CIA officials under surveillance. Andreas played a role similar to Bobby Kennedy's when Jack Kennedy was president.

When we went to Greece, I heard about the movie "Z," and also the movie "Zorba." Both were banned by the Greek government. The movie "Z" was about the Lambrakis affair— the murder of popular left-wing Deputy George Lambrakis by right-wing political goons.

When we arrived in Greece three or four weeks after the April 21 *coup d' etat*, we began hearing about Andreas. On that night of April 21, he had been arrested and hauled off to jail. Since he was suspicious of the KYP and the CIA, he didn't always sleep at home, but that night he made a mistake—he went home. He was under constant surveillance, and that night his home and the entire block was surrounded by the Greek secret police who banged on his front door. When no one answered, they broke the door down and entered the house. After searching all over, they failed to find him, but knew he had gone in but hadn't come out. They took his oldest son, George, outside and put a gun on him and yelled they would kill him if Andreas didn't come out. That excited Andreas, and he came sliding down the rain drain, fell, and hurt one of his legs. His body guards had lifted him up onto the roof of the house.

Most of the Americans at the American Embassy knew Andreas, but Ray and I had never heard of him. They said he was a liberal democrat. After his arrest, his wife, Margaret, hastened to the American Embassy and asked for intervention. He was an American citizen, and so were his wife and children!

The official Americans in Athens saw Andreas as a traitor and renegade. Things were always volatile between Greece and Turkey, and they were both vital to the southern flank of NATO. Greece was agitated over the Cyprus situation and was constantly wanting to go to war. If Papandreou won the election for prime minister, there would be a military coup. Andreas considered the Greek military his enemies. The military was aware of the situation, and they were getting nervous and itchy. The Palace, the ERE, hard core, the military and the conservative establishment were determined they would not permit Papandreou to come to power.

One day I overheard my son, Timmy, saying to his younger brother, Rusty, "Go play with Andy and Nicky. No one will play with them any more." They only lived up the street and around the corner. One day I came home and there were two little boys in my house with Timmy and Rusty. Timmy introduced me to Andy and Nicky. After they left, I asked Timmy who they were, and he said they were the little Papandreou boys. I asked Timmy if he knew where their father was, and he said yes. Tim said he was in prison. I asked if he knew why their father was in prison, and he said he was in prison because he was going to be the next president of Greece.

Later, Tim was invited to a birthday party at their home. I asked what he saw and heard. He said there was a large bulletin board in the kitchen. On the bottom of the bulletin board there was a black and white photograph of Mr. and Mrs. Papandreou at dinner with something handwritten on the bottom. It said, "Last night of freedom." Many times Timmy would be there while Margaret was preparing to leave for prison to visit Andreas. He said she always took cigarettes and whiskey with her. When she returned from her visit with

Andreas, she would rush to the American Embassy and insist they must intervene because the junta was threatening to execute Andreas.

Since Ambassador Phillips Talbot was not in good standing with the junta, someone else had to do the intervening. Orders had come from President Lyndon B. Johnson to intervene on behalf of Andreas because he was an American citizen. Ray was the one who was tapped to visit the junta about the release of Andreas. He told them that many people in the American Embassy didn't like him any better than they did, but if they executed him, he would be the martyr, and they would be the villains. But, if they released and exiled him, they would be the heroes. So they released and exiled him.

We heard he went to Canada for safe haven, and there he began his campaign against the military regime in Greece. Both he and Melina Mecouri launched a campaign against the government of Greece. Both were declared *persona non grata*. Melina was married to Jules Dassin, who was a communist, and she was also a communist.

Many other well known Greeks had managed to flee the country during the military overthrow. The ones who remained said they were "free" Greeks inside the borders of Greece. There were many arrests and detainments of high-level civilian and military officers. There were rumors of torture and even death in some cases.

CHAPTER 14

American Embassy Diplomatic Duty

ONCE A MONTH, Mrs. Talbot had a protocol coffee. The embassy had seventeen senior wives, and we had to arrive at the residence precisely at 9:30 A.M.—not a minute earlier, and not a minute later. When we arrived, we went directly into the study where Mrs. Talbot, Marjorie McClelland, wife of the *charge d' affairs*, Patsy Eaton, wife of the JUSMAAG general, and the CIA station chief's wife were all sitting on the sofa. The sofa was reserved for the ranking wives, and we knew better than ever to sit there. We all sat, round robin, in straight chairs in front of them. Mrs. Talbot would talk to us and always asked what we had been doing the past month. I was nervous and did not know exactly what she wanted to know. Ray and I were so busy every night going to different parties, and I didn't feel like digging into every little detail about our activities. I could not understand why she wanted to know what we had been doing. I always felt like if there was something important that the ambassador needed to know, Ray could tell him at his monthly meeting in the security room, the plastic bubble that hung from the ceiling in the embassy. Sometimes I felt like I was still a student nurse. But even in nursing school I had not been treated in such a juvenile manner.

Before the meeting was over, Mrs. Talbot would tell the JUSMAAG general's wife she could leave the room so she could speak in private to just her embassy wives. This made the general's wife angry. Actually, the same procedure was followed at the ambassador's meeting with his embassy officials. The general and his wife could sit in on the meetings and brief the ambassador and his wife about their business, but when they were asked to leave the room, they could not understand. But what they didn't understand was that we were state department and they were merely military. They were being treated according to protocol, but it was a bit rough on them, and they did not like military attachés. Another grievance was that State Department military attachés had diplomatic license tags on their cars and mere military had ordinary tags. I, myself, thought it was a gratuitous annoyance and one that should have been resolved so that the resulting hard feelings could have been avoided.

The Air Force attaché's wife and I were close friends. When we had to attend Mrs. Talbot's coffees, we took turns driving. At the coffees, coffee and tea were served as a matter of course. Also served were martinis, Manhattans, bloody Marys, Scotch, vodka and orange juice. I guess if someone wanted something else, that too would have been made available. My friend drank so much and so often and had so much fun at these coffees, I thought it was dangerous to ride home with her behind the wheel. I suggested that we have our husbands' chauffeurs drive us, and she agreed.

At these coffees, Mrs. Talbot instructed us that we were

there to entertain her guests and that we were to circulate. She said we could only talk to one person for three minutes and no longer. If she caught you with one person longer, she would ease by you, stick a finger in your back and mumble, "Circulate!" She also instructed us to inform our husbands that at receptions she and the ambassador drank Scotch and soda. They were never to be empty handed. Also, we had to keep an eye on both of them, and if we saw someone dominating them, we were to walk up and say, "Good evening," and give them the opportunity to break away.

Mrs. Talbot loved to see a beautiful party. In December 1968, some ships of our Sixth Fleet docked at the Port of Piraeus. She arranged for their Navy band to play for a dance at the residence. Our invitations stated it would be black tie and long gown. She had her wish and was able to see the large living room converted to a dance floor filled with beautiful, variously colored long gowns. I must admit it was vibrant with color.

Aristotle Onassis and his new wife, Jacqueline, were invited to this affair, but they did not come. I did get a chance to see her one day, however, at the Athens Hilton. It was during a lunch Ray and I were having with a Greek general and his wife. The general said, "Rue, don't look now, but that is Jackie sitting over there having lunch." That is as close as I got to meeting her, and she was stunning. She was also surrounded by bodyguards.

The fast life continued. In 1968, Lyndon Johnson decided not to run again, and that meant Phillips Talbot, a political appointee of Johnson's, had to resign. Roswell McClelland, the *charge d' affairs*, became acting ambassador until President Nixon appointed a new one.

Ray was not only attending to his duties as attaché, but he was also studying for his master's degree from the University of Southern California at night at the U.S. Athena Air Base. He was also president of the board of education at the American Academy. Mrs. Talbot wanted someone from the embassy to have that job, so it was arranged. Because he had to go to school three or four evenings a week, I had to go to many of the cocktail parties and receptions alone. Samos, our chauffeur, took me and waited outside. I would go through the receiving lines, and when people asked about Ray, I would say he was parking the car and would be here in a minute. Then, I would take a drink and greet the key people and slip out and go to the next party and do the same thing over and over. By the third party, Ray would catch up with me, and then we would go to an official dinner at 9:00 P.M. I do not think anyone ever knew I went alone to so many parties.

But, that was just part of the job. I kept telling myself that over and over.

One morning at about 5:00 o'clock, in June 1969, I awoke to the constant ringing of a telephone. I was in a deep, deep sleep, and it seemed to me it had been ringing for a long time. When I picked up the phone and said hello, it was Alice Papageorgiou. She was crying and said Dinos had been arrested by the secret police at 3:00 o'clock in the morning. He had not been allowed to take anything but what he was sleeping in and his shoes. She did not know where they had taken him.

She was desperate. I reached over and hit Ray with my fist. I wanted him awake in a hurry, and he was in a sound sleep. The first thing he said was, "Tell her not to bring George home from Cornell." George was due to arrive in

Athens in two days for his summer vacation.

I told her I would come to her penthouse that morning, and then our telephone lines were cut. Before this, when friends had been arrested by the junta, they and their families just disappeared and no one saw or heard from them again. During breakfast, I told Ray I was going to see Alice and try to find out what happened to Dinos. I made up my mind I was not going to lose these good friends. I didn't care what anyone in the embassy thought—not even the ambassador.

Ray told me to go in our private car. He didn't want our chauffeur, Samos, to be involved because we never knew for certain whether or not he was being paid by the junta for information on us. They didn't trust anyone, and we didn't trust anyone. Ray said I should drive around the block of the penthouse, and if I saw anyone across the street, to just keep on going. I put some cold beer, cokes, nuts and chips into a paper bag and drove myself to the penthouse. A Greek military jeep was parked directly across the street, so I parked a block away and walked with my paper bag directly to the penthouse and up the steps. When the military police saw me coming, they backed up very slowly around the corner. I went up the steps and entered the apartment complex, pushed the bell to her penthouse, and rode up in the elevator. When I entered the apartment, I was completely aghast! The mess! I had never seen anything like it! The secret police had literally torn up the place looking for anything and everything—papers, weapons, anything they could accuse Dinos of having in his possession.

We drank a beer and talked. I told her to call George at Cornell and tell him not to come back to Greece for now. The junta might snatch his passport and not let him leave Greece to return to the United States to complete his studies at

Cornell. She was so scared. She said if she called him, the junta would monitor it. She asked Ray and me to get in touch with him. She did not want to get arrested too.

When I left her, I stopped at the embassy to see Ray and told him what I had seen and what Alice had told me. She did not know where the secret police had taken Dinos. She was calling around to friends and to some of Dinos' peers.

That evening we had to attend a dinner with members of the junta at a seaside restaurant at Glyfada. I remember how I stared at them as we were eating. I was mad and when the music played and I had to dance with one of them, I was revolted. It isn't easy to be polite and cordial to people we don't like and fear, but we did get through the evening. As soon as dinner was over, we had our plans. We decided we would not use any telephone lines from within the embassy. It was too easy for the junta to intercept messages to and from the embassy. We went directly to a secure place near Glyfada where we felt we could have a safe, direct communication with Washington, D.C.

At Glyfada, Ray made a call to Air Force Colonel Herb Rosenthal, who had been the former air attaché to Athens, and had just returned to duty at the Defense Intelligence Agency in Washington. He agreed to make contact with George at Cornell. The message for George was not to return to Greece under any circumstances until he heard from "Rue." We told him his father was living in a hotel and his mother was OK. This was our code for telling him his father had been arrested.

Then we contacted Alice and let her know George got the message. She finally located Dinos. He was being detained in a prison near Athens. She was not allowed to get close to him.

She had to stand back a distance, and they had to yell at each other in order to be heard. He told her not to let George come back to Greece.

Alice had no idea what to do now. Her husband was a political prisoner and her son was in the United States. We arranged to send American dollars to George to help him until other arrangements could be made.

Ray arranged a meeting with General Vassilios Tsoumbas, Chief of Staff of the Greek Armed Forces. We had dinner at a seaside restaurant, and Ray and the general went for a walk on the beach. That was the only sure way for privacy.

Ray asked the general if he could do anything for Dinos, but the general said he was really sorry and he would love to help, but if he made any attempt to rescue Dinos, he himself would be arrested.

Nothing could be done, and we also had to be careful. Any overt signs of interference and we, too, could be declared *persona non grata* and be forced to leave the country at once.

Junta Rule by Terror

WE LOVED GREECE and the Greek people. Most of them were honest, hard working, and lived the lifestyle of Americans more than any country we ever lived in. The women were beautiful and the men good looking. Most of the men were good dancers. It was hard to live in a country and like the people so much but realize it was ruled by terror. Greece was "The Cradle of Democracy," but there was no democracy under the rule of the military regime. Before the overthrow of the government on April 21, 1967, old gray-haired men loved to sit at a table outside a tavern, smoke, drink coffee and talk politics. Now they had to be careful where they talked and what they said, or they might have ended up being arrested and tortured.

Our government had placed sanctions on the military regime and withheld a lot of military aid to Greece. Some of our congressmen demanded a total ban of any kind of aid to Greece. They were concerned because of rumors of mistreatment and actual torture of high-level Greek citizens and military prisoners. One American congressman demanded that the U.S. Government withhold all aid to Greece, a country ruled by terror. At receptions and cocktail parties among the many different foreign embassies, there were always whispers and rumors floating around about someone being arrested and detained and never seen again. Some American congressmen came to Athens to try to find out what was going on and returned to the U.S. to say we should not hand over American taxpayers' money to a government that ruled by terror.

What kinds of torture? Who were the prisoners? In Athens, they were businessmen, priests, Army officers, lawyers, housewives and students. The torture took place at the big prison called Asphalia Headquarters, in downtown Athens on Bouboulinas Street. Asphalia is the name of the Greek security police who raced around in small black unmarked cars and made their arrests at 3:00 A.M. when most people were asleep. They would hustle their prisoners up to the roof of the building, tie them down on a wooden bench, and pound them on the soles of their dangling feet with a shovel handle. This technique was called "falanga." At Bouboulinas Street, the shoes are left on. It is extremely painful because swelling feet eventually pop the shoes apart. When it became so painful that the victim began to scream, someone would hoist a urine-soaked rag from a toilet hole and jam it inside their mouth. Also, there were motorcycles parked outside the building on the street and someone would start the motors and rev them so loud no one could hear the screaming from the roof. If the victim became nauseated and vomited, he was forced to get on the floor and lick it up. This torture was called "The Machine of Truth."

Falanga was the basic torture. In Athens, the victim was tied to a bench or chair. In Salonika, he was stripped below the waist and laid on his back with his feet between the sling and stock of an American M-1 rifle. They would hoist the rifle, twisting it to immobilize his feet, and someone would slam away at the exposed soles. The pain feels like an electric shock. Finally, the legs would swell and the victim urinated blood. Sometimes they were given a forced enema with household detergent, and then the torturers boasted that they would pull the victim's bowels out through his mouth.

My good friend, Alice Papageorgiou, said to me, "I can't understand why Americans want democracy in their country but smile upon people who destroy democracy in my country. Democracy is not just for the Americans."

I stayed close to Alice, and every time she was allowed to go to the prison to see Dinos, she came to see me. She had to take him food, because if she didn't, he did not eat. She usually took him a whole boiled chicken because it lasted longer. But she was not allowed to see him. I told her if it was my husband, I would wonder if he got the food. The next time she went, I suggested she ask the guards for permission to write him a note and allow him to answer. If they refused, I would put the food down and yell his name as loud as I could and see what happened. Of course, I said she would be taking a chance—they might arrest her too. They refused, and she did what I suggested. She yelled his name and he answered her. He asked her to bring him a blanket because he was underground sleeping on a cold concrete floor.

In Athens, all of the foreign embassies made an agreement to reserve Sundays for family day. One Sunday, we took Debby, Timmy, and Rusty to an American movie in Kifissia. Son Don had his own plans. When we arrived home after the movies and opened the front door, he was sitting on the love seat using the telephone. He was surprised and hung up the phone immediately and said, "I thought you were upstairs! Someone was walking around up there!" We spread out and all ran in different directions but found no one. Upstairs, all of the windows and French doors opening out to balconies were locked from the inside. We never did find out who was upstairs and how they managed to get out, undetected, but sometime later I decided they must have slipped up into the attic until we were asleep.

When I took Alice to lunch after visiting Dinos in prison, I asked her questions. Was he tortured? She suspected he was, but wasn't positive. She knew other prisoners had been. I asked how they were tortured, and it was then she told me about the falanga. I asked if she knew who the torturers were. "Yes," she said. She told me the director was Basile Lambrou. I took notes as she talked. Those working for Lambrou who actually carried out the tortures were Odyssef Spanos, Constantine Karapanayiotis, and Basile Gravaritis, among others. There were many other methods too numerous and grotesque to mention, such as beatings and electricity applied to certain parts of the body. I was depressed and sad about the whole situation, and even though I had no reason not to believe Alice, it was hard to believe the people we were social-izing with nearly every night could condone such things.

One morning after Ray and I had breakfast, I noticed a man on a scaffold outside a window at the end of the hall next to the kitchen. I wondered if we were having some work done outside the house. When I picked up the phone to call Ray to find out, the whole cord came through. It was just dangling. The man on the scaffold became excited and spoke to me very fast in Greek. All I could understand was that he made a mistake. I asked him to fix it back fast. With heavy black electrical tape, he put it back together. I called Ray, and in a short time, someone from the embassy arrived. By the time they got there, the man and the scaffolding were gone. Security cleaned out the line and told me they could only guarantee us a clean line for two weeks at a time. It didn't make any difference. We knew our line was tapped and never talked about anything confidential anyway.

In June, 1969, Evans and Novak came to Athens. They came to the American Embassy and wanted to interview the U.S. Army attaché. They knew he had a close relationship with the junta. Ray's superiors advised him to refuse the interview. They wanted to keep our relationship with the junta as smooth as possible because Greece was a very important base for NATO. We all had to be careful and weigh every word we said in conversations with the Greeks. One mistake and you could be declared *persona non grata* and ordered to leave the country within twenty-four hours.

Even so, Evans and Novak wrote an article about the military regime, which was published in the International Herald Tribune June 19, 1969.

The Greek military dictatorship, after two years of empty assurances to Washington about restoring democracy, intended to retain power indefinitely without free elections—posing immense danger to long-range stability in the strategic Eastern Mediterranean.

Car Bombing and Farewell to Greece

O NE NIGHT in early July 1969, Ray and I were invited to dinner at a Greek tavern by three generals who were in good standing with the junta. No one ate dinner before 10:00 P.M., so we didn't return home until about 2:00 A.M. As we were getting ready for bed, we heard a loud "boom." Our car had been bombed! Both cars were parked on the street because the gate was too small to bring them through. Someone had driven by slowly and tried to roll a bomb underneath. The entire left side of the car looked like it had been machine gunned, and the gas tank was full of holes.

The next morning, the streets were flooded with leaflets stating that Colonel Raymond Francisco Savario Aquilina, the Army attaché, had been spoken to with bombs. The next time they would kidnap and execute him for his cozy relationship with the military regime of Greece. The Seventeenth of November Terrorist Group spoke and took credit for the bombing. We had no idea how someone managed to know the name on Ray's birth certificate. No one else knew it. He was only known as Raymond Francis Aquilina. This particular terrorist group was made up of Greek, Libyan, Jordanian and perhaps other Mideastern nationalities. There had been numerous bombings around Athens. Cars of our Air Force personnel had been bombed; foreign air line offices, and American Express buildings had been bombed. The terrorists decided they wanted more publicity, and they figured by hitting someone from the American Embassy, they would get the publicity they wanted. They were right.

After the bombing of our car, the Greek government placed twenty-four hour around-the-clock security on our house. A large guard stood at the front gate with a machine gun. When we had a dinner party, two guards were assigned to sit in the kitchen, and the entire block was surrounded by Greek military police. If anyone appeared suspicious, their car was searched.

Ambassador and Mrs. Talbot left Athens and the new ambassador and his wife arrived. There were so many parties we had to check with protocol so as not to conflict with each other's parties. The naval attaché gave a formal sit down dinner with the top Greek naval officers, and the air and Army attachés did the same.

Mrs. Traca, the new ambassador's wife, was nice, and we found out she would be easy to work with. She didn't care anything about women's clubs and also did not like the decor in the embassy residence. She went back to Rome and stayed until the residence was completely redecorated to her taste. Taxpayers never dream that some of their monies go to please high-ranking diplomats serving overseas.

Our tour was over in May 1970, and things were very busy. Also, one more trip was in store for us. Ray always wanted me to travel with him, and I usually did, but this time I didn't want to go off and leave Timmy and Rusty alone with just the servants. Ray told the ambassador, and he arranged to have security from the embassy stay at our house with the children.

So we took the trip. We spent the night in Trikala and attended a cocktail party and dinner. The next day, we visited another Greek military installation. Then, the third day, we put the car on a ferry over to Corfu for a two-day visit. We stayed in a beautiful hotel where there was a casino. I had never been in a casino before. As a matter of fact, I didn't know how to gamble, but everyone was gambling and seemed to be having a great time. I played the slots and didn't have much luck, so I moved on to the roulette table. I watched the winners at the roulette table and put my money on the same number and won a little. Or, should I say, I didn't break the bank.

During the spring of 1970 we were busy going to parties and getting ready to leave Greece. A month before our departure, we vacated our house and moved into the American Club in Kifissia.

Ray had orders for his new assignment back in the States. He was to be head of the Army R.O.T.C. at the University of Missouri in Columbia. He originally requested the University of Arkansas because the twins, Danny and Debby, were there, but Colonel Holmes already had that job. Remember him? He was the one who had to deal with Bill Clinton regarding the draft.

We had our farewell reception around the pool at the American Club where we were staying. Our children told their friends that Vice President Syllianos Pattakos would be there, and they didn't believe them. All of the children lingered around, watching and waiting, when suddenly they heard sirens. It was the Vice President being escorted by the police.

On the morning of our departure, there was a big party at the airport to say goodbye. Ray had to drag me on the plane. I had too much champagne, and also I was scared to death to fly—especially over the ocean!!

At Kennedy International Airport, we breezed through customs with our diplomatic passports. That's when we woke up to the realization that the icing on the cake was over. I always had a philosophy. For a good assignment, I always said, "I am going from the sink to the mink." Now it's over, and I'm going from the mink back to the sink.

Afterword

WHEN OUR TOUR in Athens was over, we found Ray's next assignment very dull and boring after the fast jet-set life. He was assigned as Professor of Military Science at the University of Missouri in Columbia. Since it would be his last assignment, we began looking around for a retirement home, and decided on El Paso, Texas. We moved into our new home in January 1973, and Ray took a job with a financial management corporation. He was successful, and with this corporation came several interesting trips.

In October 1974, we took a trip to Madrid. Afterward, we flew over to Athens and had a reunion with dear old friends. The military regime had been toppled, and all political prisoners were released, and all members of the junta were thrown in jail. We have had the chance to return to Athens four times, but the last time was a disappointment. Things never stay the same.

Despite being just a little ordinary girl from Arkansas, I've had a good and interesting life. I've lived in a lot of places and in several foreign countries. I don't know why I was put on this earth, but I hope I've served my country well. It isn't everyone who has the chance to know when their usefulness has run out, but I'm the lucky one. I'm lucky because I had a good husband who gave me five beautiful and healthy children, which resulted in four beautiful grandchildren. He is the one who made it possible for me to have such a rich and interesting life. He made everything possible for me. We both worked hard to make a good life for ourselves, our children, and our beautiful grandchildren. It has been a fulfilling journey from start to finish. Goodbye.